LYRIC PSALMS:
HALF A PSALTER

LYRIC PSALMS: HALF A PSALTER

Francis Patrick Sullivan

The Pastoral Press
National Association of Pastoral Musicians
225 Sheridan St. NW
Washington, DC 20011

ACKNOWLEDGMENTS

The Bible Today	Psalms 22, 23, 26, 66, 91, 95, 100, 145
New Catholic World	Psalms 1, 8, 42, 43
	"Spiritual Imagery: Some Rules"
Liturgy	Psalms 102, 103
Pulpsmith	Psalm 104
The Denver Quarterly	Oratorio For An Apocalypse
Concilium	"Psalm Translation: Creating A New Poem"

Book design and cover design
by Aileen Callahan

ISBN 0-9602378-8-7

The Pastoral Press
225 Sheridan Street NW, Washington, DC 20011
(202) 723-5800

The Pastoral Press is the publications division of The National Association of
Pastoral Musicians, a membership organization of musicians and clergy
dedicated to fostering the art of musical liturgy.

Drawings by Aileen Callahan
© 1982 Aileen Callahan

CONTENTS

DRAWINGS BY AILEEN CALLAHAN

FOR MARGARET

FOR   JEREMIAH

Foreword

I worked on the selection of psalms that follows with the lyric imagination I use for my own poetry. I tried for a new act of creation to match the ancient one. My basic text was Mitchell Dahood's Anchor Bible Psalms. I chose Dahood not for his sense of English language, but for his sense of imagery and poetry at play in the original texts. I admire his work deeply for that reason. The English language I use comes from contemporary poetry, my own and that of others whom I read and teach. Most of the psalm versions in this book are done to a syllable count line in order to catch the flavor of the ancient style with a modern one, to give musicians a stable pattern to work with, and lectors a floating pattern of accents for vivid delivery, and to give readers tight phrases to recall if they wish. There are two essays following the psalms. One appears in *Concilium*, an issue on the creative tradition in liturgy. The other appears in *New Catholic World*, an issue on creativity and religious experience. The two essays give the best explanation I can make of what I intended to do in this work on the psalms. In the last section of the volume, there is a poem, *Oratorio For An Apocalypse*, which originally appeared in *The Denver Quarterly*, and an explanation of it. It is in with these psalms and essays because it is the mother-lode of my poetic imagination and may help to explain also how I work. The illustrations of the psalms were made at my request by Aileen Callahan. She had worked up this abstract style earlier, for a set of Stations Of The Cross. I appreciate her work deeply. I hope that the two arts together will honor the psalms with lyrical language and lyrical line. I offer here my profound gratitude to Burton Raffel, poet, translator, critic, a dear friend of my poetry and myself. My thanks to Carroll Stuhlmueller, CSP, and also to The MacDowell Colony which gave me a residency to complete this project.

PSALMS

PSALM 1

What grace!
never to be partner
to a crime
nor thick with the lawless
or cynics,
but able to be with God
law by law
night and day eagerly,
like that tree
someone moves near water
so it blooms.
It stays fruitful and green.
It stays good,
not like chaff, criminals
blown away.
The two will never mix.
Tree and chaff
in the end part company.
God will keep
only fruits of justice
forever.
The rest will blow downwind.

PSALM 4

I need You now
    to answer me, O God!
You have before,
    freed me from disaster!
Think how I need
    You now, free me again!

You insult God,
    you powers that be, my
beautiful God,
    you traffic with nothings
who tell you lies!
    You need to know
that God rewards belief
    with miracles,
that God will answer me!
    Yes, fear for rain,
but no sin! Know your soul!
    Know your sorrow!
Offer yourselves cleanly
    and trust to God!
Yes, you say, who
    will give rain? The good will
of God is gone!

    I want the joy
of seeing You grow wheat
    and wine for them.
I sleep easy in Your
    presence, Your peace!
Only in You do I
    feel such release!

PSALM 6

You are angry at me.
You punish me.
Please stop, I am worn out.
Stand in my place.
I am hurt to the bone,
my soul a bruise.
Will you keep after me?
Change, please, cure me,
save me, You are not harsh.
Can a dead mouth
know what to sing for praise?
I cry myself
to sleep, no song, so tired,
my pillow damp,
I darken what I see,
deaden my heart.
I know my tears reach You.
Death has no hold.
You take these words from me.
You accept me.
You shake death loose from me.
You bury it.

Psalm 8

PSALM 8

God, our God,
Your name is beautiful
everywhere.
You will hear me prattle
it, babble
it beyond everywhere,
beautiful!
You made Your sky a strength
when You beat
Your worst enemies, hate
and revenge.
When I see how the sky
moon and stars
flow from Your fingertips,
what are we,
childrens' children, that You
bring us up,
not as demi-gods, but
little less,
as those You can honor
and respect,
charged with creation,
its carpet
of beasts, big, small, wild, tame,
birds aloft,
fish below crisscrossing
the sea roads,
God, our God, beautiful,
everywhere!

PSALM 13

Will You forget me, God?
How long? For good?
Will You look away, God?
How long? How long?
I live the soul of doubt,
the heart of tears.
Must death fool with me?
How long? Look! Speak!
Lift my eyelids, O God!
Sleep is deadly.
Death will crow if it wins,
"I ate him up!"
You are the kind I trust.
I know You help.
I will crow if You do,
"God is lavish!"

PSALM 14

They are stupid
who do hideous things
because there is no God,
there is no good.
Heaven watches
every human being.
God can see even one
who looks upward.
Not one of them
is moral—all stupid
apart, together all
corrupt—not one!
Can they ignore
that they eat what belongs
to God when they gorge on
God's own people.
Look at that pack.
God is with its victims.
The killers are the fools,
not the victims.
Let Zion bear
new life, let God remake
Israel, let Jacob
be fat with joy.

PSALM 15

Who is welcome
with You, God, who can live
   above with You?
Someone honest, someone
   just, someone who
speaks to reveal the heart;
   no one who lies,
no one who damages
   others, no one
who smirches a good name.
   Such like are not
welcome, but someone is
   to Your feasting
who follows Your commands,
   someone who wills
firmly to do no wrong,
   no usury,
no living off the poor!
   Such like will make
no mistake where they go!

PSALM 16

O God, keep me!
I came to You to stay alive.
I professed it,
You are my God, You have no match.
The local gods
and powers who once charmed me can
suffer for it:
stretch their birth pangs out, stretch their lust.
I will not use
my hands or lips to pour them wine
or say their names.
You pour me wine, O God, You smooth
my life ahead.
You draw the lines so I own fields
of loveliness.
I credit You with teaching me
right from the heart
even in the dead watch of night.
I fix on You.
I will not dodge Your directions.
My heart is full
of joy, my flesh is ecstatic
to be alive.
You will not damn me, You will not
make me watch death,
but know the way, the lasting life
of joy You give,
the endless pleasure close to You.

Psalm 19

PSALM 19

You made a glory of
    space, it glows with Your touch!
Daylight teaches daylight,
    darkness teaches darkness,
voicelessly, wordlessly,
    soundlessly, mouth to mouth!
Your glories fill the earth
    to the brim with their call
to the sun in its tent
    to rise from bed, a groom,
and run the sky clanging
    its shield with defiance,
arcing rim to rim but
    never missing its bride!
The way You order things
    freshens the soul in me.
The stable patterns You
    set are strokes of genius.
Your rules to live by are
    so fair my heart fills up,
the sunlight of Your law
    that gives me eyes to see,
a pure light, a lasting
    light issuing from You,
a pure truth, pure justice
    every time You judge us.
I want Your judgments more
    than stacks of bullion gold.
They are sweeter to me
    than honey from the comb.
I see my way by them,
    I watch them bring me life!

I err, who knows why, You
   will have to forgive me!
You will have to protect
   me from idolaters.
They could control my soul.
   If You do, I will stay
clean of the one great sin!
   I want to match my words
to Yours, my deepest thoughts
   to what You want for me,
God, my ground, my glory!

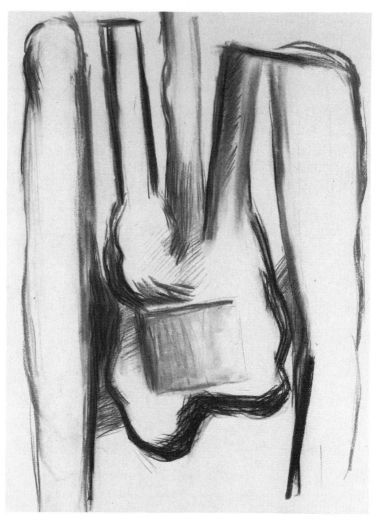

Psalm 22

PSALM 22

God, God,

why have You dropped me cold,
cut off from You, echo-less,
my words stuck in my throat
dumb days and sleepless nights.

Our elders called You Holy
Enthroned, Israel's Praise,
said trust You, trust You,
You cut off no one, left
no one shouting for nothing.

I must be some worm
jeered at by an ugly mob,
"Crawl to God to save you!
See if God cares for worms!"

You were midwife for me.
You kept me at her breast.
You own me from her body.
You must not leave me bare,

bullied and bitten by tongues
wagging in fierce mouths.

I am drained, disjointed
by fear, it burns me down,
dries me to my lips,
down to the dust of death.

They dog me with their crimes,
I feel them at my bones,
thugs who pick me clean,
who throw dice for my clothes.

(over)

Do not stay aloof.
Hurry, help me, God!
Do not leave me as meat
or drink for beasts of war.
Pull me out of horror!
Pull me free of carnage!

Then I can tell my people
when they flock to know You:

hold to God, cheer
God for joy, you chosen!
Victims move that face!
Victims touch that heart!

I owe you my own praise
in this believing crowd.
The poor shall eat their fill.
The God-fearing respond,
"Live your hearts forever!"

The earth remembers care.
All races pray for it.
You rule oppression out!
You rule the strongman out!

Death dusts all our heads!

My soul, my young, will live
our future proclaiming You,
the God who makes us whole!

PSALM 23

A shepherd and one sheep
my God and I,
my field, my well, my soul
alive and full,

my sinless way
through crimes that shadow me
with hills of death
out of a shepherd's care,

You, my sturdy weapon,
my steady pace
to where You wait on me
as hate looks on,
my balm, my brimming drink,

so love will track
my life with loyal steps
right to Your door,
my home, my final days.

PSALM 24

God owns the earth,
   owns its richness,
      owns its peoples.

God made it stand
   fathoms deep in
      chaotic seas!

Then who is fit
   to mount to God,
      to God's temple
         to stand and pray?

Clean hands, clean hearts,
   who never once
      reached for idols
         to swear an oath!

God will grace you!
   God will give you
      a richer life!

Look for a live
   God, look for a
      living presence!

You gates of God
   lean back, lean back,
      loud with your joy,
         your glory comes!

Do you know who?

God, who fought with
chaos and won!

Lean back, you gates,
you gates of God,
loud with your joy,
your glory comes!

Do you know who?

Your god, who owns
the world, who owns
its glory, all!

PSALM 26

Prove me right to choose
You as my rule.
Probe my heart and see
You are my law.

No cheat, no liar
is my hero,
You are, Your love is,
I bask in it,
singing, parading
the good You do.

I love the beauty
of Your altar.

Do not judge me one
with people's greed;
they dirty their hands
as I will not.

Get me free of them!

I will stand up
and bless You every
time we worship.

PSALM 27-A

God is living light
to me; God is a wall
that frees my life from fear;
no one else can touch it!
They die first, the ones who
are thirsty for my blood,
the ones who oppose me
mortally, they die first!
If an army of them
shows to level my life,
I will not fear it,
so much do I trust God.
I prayed God for one thing
so often I forget:
to live out my whole life
in this place where God comes,
so lovely to my eyes
when I wake up at dawn.
When I die, I will be
dear to God where God lives,
in the sky, in a tent,
or up on a mountain,
my life well beyond reach
of earthly enemies.
I will make holy all
that is holy, shouting,
dancing, singing, for God!

(over)

PSALM 27-B

I need You to listen.
I need You to answer.
O God, I need You to.
I want to see Your face.
It is this love I have.
It makes me search for You.
Do not avoid my eyes
or let me anger You.
Do not toss me aside.
O God, do not drop me.
You are the only hope
I have; father, mother,
they can leave me orphaned,
but Your love must never.
Lead me to You, O God,
along the smoothest road.
There are those who hate me.
Do not leave me to them.
They eat my life away
by lying under oath
or twisting evidence.
I trust Your love. I will
see Your beauty after
death in Your land of life.
My love will wait for You.
It will be strong waiting.
O God, my love will wait!

Psalm 29

23

PSALM 29

Applaud,
little gods, applaud
your God,
you owe your glory!
Bow low
when The Holy looms,
the voice
looms in from the sea,
God, God,
booming in thunder,
God, loose,
out, over the deep,
strong voice,
power itself, bright
voice, light
itself, loose from God,
splitting
cedars to splinters,
cedars
of Lebanon, God's sharp
blows are
licks of fire, down, down,
they bounce
the earth, bounce the hills
like beasts,
wild, skipping oxen.
Thunder!
God buckles the fields.
Thunder!
God labors the deer
and bares
the forests of leaves.

Thunder!
God's temple flares up,
flares with
visions of glory!
The throne
of God since chaos,
the throne
of God forever!
God, God,
maker of triumph,
God, God,
of chaos and peace!

PSALM 30

I want the world to know
You drew me up
like water from the well
of death, O God,
when death had almost won.
O God, my God,
I was on my last breath
when You healed me,
hauled me up from the well
I headed down.
I want the world to sing
Your holy name.
Your anger would kill us,
Your love save us,
as tears would make us sleep,
and joy wake us.
I was carefree, never
thought about death.
Your love made me stronger
than hills, O God.
When You took it away,
I shook with fear.
I said: Will You listen,
will You help me!
Why wring tears out of me!
Why watch me die!
The slime of death is mute,
its mouth is shut
about You, God, hear me!
Have some pity,
Will You help me instead!
Make my tears turn

dance, my penance turn joy!
Make my heart sing,
free of death, O God, my
thanks forever!

PSALM 31

I trust You, God.
It could cause my downfall.
Do not let it.
Stay faithful, set me free,
eternal God!

Listen now or never,
You must be quick,
hold me, my mountain God,
my fortress God,
my rock cliff, my strong wall!

It is Your own
dignity that guides You.
It will guide me.
You will disentangle
me from any
net concealed to trap me.
I trust You to.
You will ransom my life.
I ask You to,
not some senseless statues
that people use,
hateful things; I trust You
instead, Your kind
treatment of me will make
my happiness.
You saw Death turn on me.
You interfered.
You did not surrender
me to Death to
walk its endless reaches.

Will You be my
relief from all this pain!
I am dull-eyed,
hoarse, starved because of it.
It consumes me.
What life I have is grief;
it saps my strength,
it makes me skin and bones,
a bitter joke
to neighbors and to friends
a tragic fright,
they dodge me in the streets
as if I am
some stupid, shrunken corpse
or broken pot.

I know people call me
a fear monger
when they work up plans
to murder me.
I said I trusted You,
my whole life is
placed in You. I still claim
You as my God!
Loosen their grip on me,
the murderers!
Bring me out in the sun
to see Your face.
Do not make me look like
a fool, O God!
Make the wicked look like
fools stuck in hell!

(over)

Shut the mouths of liars
and those who mock
Your name for being just!

You store up so
many gifts for those who
treat You with love,
gifts for those who trust You
before the world.
You free them from slander,
You shelter them
from bitter tongues; they stay
in your presence.
Your kindness to me is
wonderful, it
comes down from Your heaven.
I am grateful.
I once despaired of You
thinking: God has
turned a blind eye to me.
But You knew that
I asked for Your mercy.

Let those who love
God know God embraces
their lives: let those
who defy God know God
defies them back.
Let those who hope in God
be strong, be brave!

PSALM 32

What peace, God,
when You forgive our sins,
what relief
when You judge we are free
of malice.
Once, I was in pieces,
skin and bone
grieving about my guilt,
night and day,
with You, God, after me
like a drought
ravaging a summer.
I let You
know I could hide no more.
I told You:
O God, I admit my sins,
God, I do!
You took away my guilt.
All of us
can ask the same of You
even if
sins are like war, like floods
we drown in.
You are my one defense
against sin.
Wrap Yourself around me,
then tell me
You will teach me to think,
to act well,
Your eye is on me now,
I am not
to play the stupid beast,
horse or mule,

(over)

You must rope and muzzle
before You
can deal with him at all.
People who
sin are buried in torment.
People who
trust You are wrapped in love.
You are joy
to all those You forgive.
We tell You,
all of us You set free.

Psalm 33

PSALM 33

Delight in God,
delight in God's charm you
lovers of God,
let it loose on a harp
so thickly strung
you can make a fresh song,
rich chords, glad chords,
for God who says and does
the strictest truth
and loves it in others,
loves being kind.
God spoke, made heaven, spoke
and peopled it,
put oceans in bottles,
fathoms in barns.
There must be world-wide awe
and love for God
who gave one order and
all this appears.
God baffles worldly plans,
worldly peoples.
God's one plan held us all
before our time,
one mind will direct things
long after it.
What a gift, to have God
single us out
from all the rest as a
personal wealth.
From the sky, from a throne
in the sky, God
pores over us all, man

woman and child,
to watch what we will make
of what we find.
Armed might does not win
for a leader,
and brute strength does not save
a follower;
one horse is no threat, one
army no help,
God spots people of truth,
be sure of it,
people who trust in love
to beat off Death
from them, ravenous Death.
We hold our souls
for God, our armed might,
the One our hearts
enjoy and care to name.
Care for us too,
O God, our life of trust!

Psalm 34

PSALM 34

I will fill God
with my gratitude each minute,
each word I say.

My voice will sound
rich in God, listen to it you
who are voiceless!

Sound rich with me saying
God's name all together.

I went begging
God and came away answered,
freed of terror.

Some just looked
to God, they shone, they will never
be made fools of.

But this beggar asked;
God heard, saved him grief.

Some angelic
force surrounds those who cherish God
to keep them free.

Drink God deeply,
the taste of sweet water, the trust
that fills the soul.

Respect God; those who do
have nothing more to ask.

Let me teach you
like children how to cherish God,

(over)

listen to me:

Who does not want life, want
time to enjoy it all?

Then bite off your tongue
before you lie or cheat.

Scorn evil, create good,
yearn for peace, search it out.

God can spot those who do.
God can hear what they want.

Cheats, liars, make God wish
to root them out for good.

God takes the cry of pain
right from innocent mouths.

God is broken with hearts
and crushed with spirits.

God frees the innocent
from all the traps of life.

God lets no one break us,
our every bone is safe.

Evil is suicide,
suicide is self-slaughter.

God pays the price for us.
We trust we will not die.

Psalm 38

PSALM 38

Please, no anger, God, it punishes me,
as if You shot at me, You struck me down.
Because of You, my whole body is sick,
and every bone I have betrays my sins.
They have become unbearable to me,
infected wounds, my own stupidities.
I am beaten. I am a walking gloom.
I burn inside, my body is unsound,
empty, empty, a moaner and groaner
in front of You, God, so You notice me,
feverish, weak, no lights to my eyes, O,
someone diseased, kept far away by friends,
by enemies trapped or hounded to death,
a malicious campaign to ruin me.
I am deaf to them, dumb to them, I hear
nothing they say, I say nothing they hear,
my ears stay closed, my mouth closed, not a word.
But Yours are not. You must answer for me
when I beg You not to let my mistakes
make me a fool in the eyes of a world
that wants to laugh. Sin is like the one who
walks beside me, sorrow is like the one
who walks ahead, my sin and my sorrow.
I have mortal enemies, powerful
and numerous. They turn the good I do
into evil and lay the blame on me.
O God, my God, do not stay so far off!
Be close to me, God, make me come alive!

PSALM 39

Watch yourself, I said,
watch your tongue, do not blame God,
the wicked enjoy
it when someone gets bitter.
I did, I shut tight,
I swallowed the pain, a mute
with no other choice,
but when I thought about it,
my anger broke out.
What becomes of me, I said,
will this go on long,
when do I vanish from sight?
Look, You made my days
only the width of my hands.
Every life is fog.
Every life is fakery,
every life a ghost
struggling with ghosts and for what!
We pile up our wealth
with no idea who gets it.
Now I am supposed
to pray: God, I hope in You!
Free me from my pain
so some fool won't laugh at me!
I kept still, I did
not beg You to change Your ways
and to stop lashing
at me like some torturer!
You punish our guilt!
You eat our guilt like a moth!
You make us a hole!
I will pray You instead, O God,

(over)

through tears on my face:
I am a guest in Your world,
so were my parents.
Forget who I am. Let me
be glad I lived. Then
let me die and do not know.

PSALM 40-A

I was near death.
God heard it in my voice,
my frantic voice.
God stooped into the slime,
hauled me back up,
then stood me on a rock,
on my own feet,
and filled my throat with a
new voice, new song.
You can see, you can hear,
you can trust God.
No one needs an empty
statue, no one
needs a magical charm.

O God, my God,
Your scope is enormous
and wonderful.
And yet You think of us
in countless ways.
I told You with this text:
"Here I am; what
I owe You is entered
beside my name,
to match my mind and heart
to Yours, O God."
I told great crowds how you
had saved my life.
You must have heard me, I
was ecstatic.
I held nothing back, how
generous You

(over)

were, how faithful, how You
acted for me,
how kind and strong You were.
I told them that
You never kept Your love
away from me,
You always kept me safe.

PSALM 40-B

I sense evils
swarming around my life;
my own sins chase
me down, I cannot run;
my head of hair,
my many sins, count them!
They stagger me!
You must come soon, O God!
You must come soon.
Those who want to kill me
or ruin me
have to be defeated
and driven off.
They have to know disgrace,
those who gloated
over me must be shamed!
Whoever loves
You should rejoice in You,
whoever finds

You should exult in You,
"Our God is great!"
I am small, I am sad,
but You see me.
Help me soon, O my God!

Psalm 42

PSALM 42

A dry doe gasps for live water—
O God, my soul for You!—
my dry soul for the living God,
when will I drown my thirst?
I drink tears instead, all the time,
hearing taunts, "Where is God?"
taunts my soul will never forget,
but bring up to God when
I cross the court and drop to pray
while people near me shout
their thanks in a holiday mood.
Why are you so sad, why
face me breathing so sad, my soul?
Wait, I can still cherish
my God, my safety, my freedom!
My soul faces me sad
because I must remember God
from a bleak gorge, a trapped
place, from mountains ringed around it,
echoes top to bottom,
strokes of thunder, lightning, rolling
waves breaking overhead.
God once sent charm to me through light
and knowledge through darkness.
This is what I will pray, "You, God,
my Rock, why forget me?
Why here, dark, death ridden, ambushed
by death in my own bones?"
Voices taunt me all day, "Where is
your God?" You, my soul, why
so sad, why breathe at me so sad?
Wait, I can still cherish
my God, my safety, my freedom!

PSALM 43

God, argue for me against them,
get me free! They believe
nothing, they trick You, profane You!
Why throw me away, You,
my one defense, God, why let them
threaten my life with death.
Brighten it instead with Your truth!
Lead me up the mountain
to Your holy place. I could walk
right in to Your altar,
my God, my joy, my life. I could
take a harp, make it sing
to You, God, my God! You, my soul,
why so sad, why breathe it
at me? Wait! I can still cherish
my God, my freedom here!

Psalm 50

PSALM 50

A summons:
God speaks it to the world
from the sun
east to west; from Sion,
pure beauty,
God rises, God sweeps in,
God must speak
like storms of fire or rain.
A summons:
God will try us before
witnesses,
heaven and earth, hear ye:
the faithful
are to rise who promised
over gifts
to be holy with God.
Hear ye: God
has a just charge to make:
listen to
me, Israel, I am
your own God
Who is accusing you:
I am here
not for gifts, not for burnt
offerings,
day in, day out; I want
no cattle
killed for me from your herds.
I own herds
in the wild, in forests,
on high crags.
I can see birds who soar
the mountains
and beasts who crawl the earth.
You cannot

know my hungers, nor you,
my whole world;
feed me no flesh, pour me
out no blood.
Keep your word, that is my
food and drink,
you, keeping faith with me.
Then, in bad
times, my faith will feed you.
Hear ye: God
says this to hypocrites:
How can you
stand to say what I love.
You hate words
about our common bond.
You compete
with thieves, you connive in
seduction,
you weave an evil spell
with your tongue,
you damn your own brothers
and sisters.
You want me to be still—
I will not!
to be evil like you—
I am not!
I blame you to your face.
Remember,
your life depends on mine.
I can feast
you forever if you
love my way.
If you keep faith with it,
I can give
you life itself to drink.

Psalm 51

PSALM 51

God, I need You,
my sins are awful things.
You are the soul
of mercy, rub them out,
the guilt of them,
wash it, wash it away,
the awful guilt,
it stares me in the face,
it is my own.
My sins hurt You the most.
I made You watch.
You have every right to
judge me harshly.
This world of sin is mine,
I am its child.
You know its shrewd deceits.
Teach me Your truths.
Make me like a well clean
of all debris,
free of sin, like someone
brighter than snow.
I need to know that joy
will follow pain.
Look past my awful sins,
make them vanish.
I ask a new conscience
from You, O God,
I ask a new courage
to keep me right.
Do not send me away
empty of You.
May I have back the joy

(over)

You saved me by,
will You bear me again
unselfishly?
I want other sinners
to turn to You.
I taste death in my tears,
O God, my God,
I want to taste a song
that honors You.
I would try offerings
on an altar,
but You do not want them,
You want my heart
sore with sorrow for sin.
Jerusalem,
make it lovely once more,
walls around it.
Then ask it to offer
on its altars
cattle it makes holy
for You alone.

Psalm 65

PSALM 65

We honor You,
O God above, in Your
deathless Sion.
Take the thanks we owe You;
You heard us pray.
We all have to face You
bearing our sins,
our countless rebel ways.
Lift them from us!

The joy of being called
by You to live
in Your temple above!
To have You fill
us with the holiness
and beauty of
Your house, O, may it be!

When You have won
our lives on the last day,
show us that time
when You made peace rule on
land and water
to their farthest reaches,
when You, with Your
own strength, steadied the
shaky mountains,
when You made the noises
of the sea still,
the quarreling waves, the
warring tribes, still,
made monsters at the edge
stock still with awe.

Shiver the stars of dawn
and dusk with joy.
Come, make a laughing earth,
thicken her trees,
fill the sky wells with water,
rain wheat on her,
you made her to bear crops!
Make her sopping,
ridge and furrow, shower
her with fresh buds,
crown her peaks with rain,
thicken her grass,
fat grass that never ends,
ribbon her hills,
dress her hollows in flocks,
shawl her valleys,
wheat for the jubilee!

PSALM 66

Shout your joy whole earth,
glory in calling God maker.

Criminals choke on Your name,
the whole of the earth sings it.

Look what God performed,
from water, dry land underfoot.

Dance there across God's eyes
who lets no rebel stand.

Thanks to God we live,
our souls are still alive.

You made us bear it, God,
smelted us, let us be trapped,
be weighted, ridden down,
run between water and fire,
then You pulled us free.

I will keep the promise
torn from me by troubles,
butcher and roast my cattle,
rams and bulls and goats,
make food my gift to You.

Listen, faithful, the story
of God I called in prayer,
"Be deaf if my heart is evil!"

God heard, heard my sound,
took it; blessed be God
who loved me without fail.

PSALM 67

Yield us grace and care,
shed your love, God, shed your light!
You alone bear life!

Let the earth know You fought for
its life. Its peoples
will embrace You as their God,
loudly, happily,
as if with a single voice!

They will follow You
to Your country, to Your land,
shouting, joyously,
honoring You, all of them!

Yield us crops here on
earth, O God, shed your blessing
on us who embrace
You, everyone, everywhere!

Psalm 71

PSALM 71

I believed You.
Do not let it make me
look like a fool!
Keep Your word, living God,
please get me free,
my life is in danger!
You promised me
Your strength, like a mountain
cliff, like a fort,
any time. Help me now!

Break the grip of
violence on me, crime
shackles my life,
You, O God, You, my hope
since I was young.
From the day my mother
labored, the day
she suckled me, You kept
me free of death.
I can never thank You!

My life was fair
game, a target, but You
helped me escape.
I spoke each day of what
You did for me
in terms glowing with praise.

I am old now.
Do not set me adrift
on failing strength.

(over)

I am still a target,
those who hate me
still want to murder me
thinking, who cares
if we kill this wretched
old fool, not God!
You, O God, You, stay close!
Help me now, please!
Let them look like the fools
they are, let them
wear their shame like a coat!

I keep my hopes
alive, I keep praying,
keep count of times
You set us free, all day,
but I lose count!

I want to stand in Your
temple, O God,
stand and say You alone
keep faith with me.
You taught me your stories
when I was young,
stories I always tell.
But old age saps
my strength; leave me enough,
O God, I want
to tell each one who comes
to this temple
what life You are to us!
Your care of us,

O God, is vast, like sky,
one of a kind!

What if You forced me through
wrong after wrong,
You keep my life in store,
You will raise me
from the deep hole of death!
My sacrifice
is for You, to ask You
to console me.

My harp, my voice, my praise
are full of You,
O God, O faithful God,
my music is full
of You, O Holy One,
my mouth is joy,
my mouth alive with song,
my soul as well,
my soul belongs to You,
my words all day,
words to tell the world
how You keep faith!

And those who want me dead!
Shame on them all!
O, scatter them away!

PSALM 72

God, give the one
who governs us Your sense
of right and wrong.
We need justice like Yours.
We are oppressed.
Make these mountains, these hills,
signal Your peace.
Make someone Your defense
of our victims,
of our famished children.
Stop their abuse.
Make someone who respects
You to the end
as the sun and moon do,
someone light as
rain on grass or desert,
who can nurture
justice and peace in us
until the moon
dries up, and rule the earth
sea to sea, end
to end, soften fierce tribes,
turn hate to dust.
Make someone all powers
in the world can
hold in awe, rich nations,
proud nations, someone
they will yield to, support.
There are the poor,
the helpless begging aid,
all the needy
whose lives draw compassion,

all the oppressed
whose blood must be precious.
May whoever
helps them live a long life
and be our wealth,
the one for whom we pray,
the one we ask
You every hour to bless
so wheat robes all
our fields, our hills give suck,
fruit trees bloom thick
like grass in Lebanon.
Let such power
last until the sun chars,
a joy to all
who must rule their people.
We honor You,
You alone, this is Your work.
It is Your name
that gives us our beauty. Amen. Amen.

PSALM 73

People of faith!
God is good for anyone who has
a clear conscience.
I nearly lost this truth, nearly
lost my balance
when I envied the arrogance
of the wicked,
their wealth, their fat and healthy looks.
They are gods on
earth, free of work, free of trouble.
They turn vicious
ways into jewelry and cloth.
They want more than
their feverish eyes can take in.
God is evil,
they say, God oppresses their world.
They bite heaven
and hell for something to chew on,
bloating like a
monster who has sucked up the sea,
and saying, Who
cares! God knows nothing about us!
It is as if
this defiance made their wealth grow,
and my attempt
at clear conscience brought me nothing,
my piety
brought me fresh trouble every day.
If I agreed
with them, I would scandalize You.
I realized
I could never know the answer

until I saw
how God would treat them after death.
You will uproot
them then like weeds so they wither.
They will be dry
as death swept off by fearful winds.
You will treat them
like ghosts from a nightmare city.
I know I soured
on You, my feelings for You stopped.
I lost my wits,
I acted like some beast You own.
But I want to
stay with You, to be lead by You
to Your heaven,
to be caught up in Your beauty.
If I am with
You, heaven is rich, earth is full.
You will give me
new flesh and blood for my decay,
God, my strong God,
the wicked will stay with their old.
Treat all those who
leave You as the nothings they are.
I have to stay
near You to be happy at all.
O God, I trust
telling people how good You are!

Psalm 74

68

PSALM 74

Why You, God, why
You in this smoking rage
at us, Your kind,
in Your field, remember?
shepherd and flock,
You named us long ago!
Fight for us now.
Fight for Your holy place.
Save Your people
buried in the rubble.
The war ruined
what is sacred to us.
Soldiers and flags
roared into Your temple,
smashed its doors down
with every ax they owned.
They gutted You
with fire, they fouled Your house.
They thought to burn
Your kind, all our people.
No sign of You!
Nothing makes sense to us!
You let this go,
this blasphemy, do You?
Do You take it,
and not move a muscle?
Why not defeat
them, God, here, in this place?
You fought the sea,
You smashed its waves rearing
their fearsome heads.
You fed sea monsters to

(over)

the desert tribes.
You made water of sand,
sand of water,
switching them back and forth.
The day, the night,
the sun, the moon are Yours!
North, south, east, west,
Yours; summer, winter, Yours!
This war curses
You blasphemes You, foolish!
Do not leave us
to these beasts; You formed us!
Do not go blind
to our pain, mighty God!
Look down at us.
Your temple, Your city,
Your fields around
are choked with violence.
We squat in shame.
We yearn to stand and praise
You, God, the one
who must defend the truth.
We plead with You.
Listen to them curse You!
They never stop!
Do not go deaf to them,
they shout louder
and louder for Your death!

PSALM 77

I am desperate, You can hear it in
my voice, God, if You would just answer me.
No, when I beg You stop, You pummel me
in the dark like someone without pity.
It hurts me to think or speak about You.
I loved to. I spent nights awake praying.
When I think what love there was between us!
All those years! Now at night, I stroke a harp
so I can heal my soul when it asks me,
is it over, is God's anger final?
Are gifts between us gone, the future gone?
Has anger shriveled God into meanness,
a withered might, a God sick with anger?
I know better. You once were a glory.
I can recite the past, wonderful things!
Your power is holy. You are supreme.
You have shown the whole world Your miracles.
Work them for us, Jacob's people, Joseph's.
There was a time, O God, there was a time
when chaotic forces, like floods loose,
shook in fear when they saw You come at them,
Your massed clouds pelting rain, Your voice booming
light zigzag cloud to cloud, thunder ringing
the sky, lightning stripping night from the earth,
shaking it to its roots. You struck a path
through those forces like rain drubbing the sea,
then leaving not a trace of Your fury
for anyone to see. Lead us after
You like the flock Moses and Aaron led.

PSALM 82

In a congress of rival gods,
one God rises to confront them:

Stop arguing for criminals!
Stop voting on the side of thugs!
Argue for the voiceless people,
cripples, orphans, victims, the poor!
Vote your criminals off their backs,
get your thugs to let people go!

The gods see nothing, know nothing,
do nothing, they look in the dark;
they kick the earth itself over.

To think of you as rival gods,
you as divine sons and daughters!
No! As men and women die, you
will die, as rulers in this world!

O God, they are gone, rise again,
fill their empty places Yourself!

PSALM 85

Grace Your arid land, Your arid
people; pardon
our sins, our guilt; stop Your anger
burning us, God!
Come to us but not in fury,
O God of grace!
Do not scorch our lives forever!
You rule the sun.
Make our lives bloom again, our joy
arise from You!
God, open up Your love to us,
make Your land grow!

I tell you God's response to this:

Yes, God will give
life to those who believe and who
open their hearts.
God will give growth to those who love.
God is glory
around us now: love will temper
law, right temper
wealth, trust will burgeon from the ground,
truth from the air,
a drenching rain will fall from God,
our crops will grow,
holiness will come, beauty come
trailing from God!

PSALM 86

You are my one hope left.
I am nearly beaten.
My life, my faith, my trust,
are Yours to keep or lose.
Stand in my place and You
will know why I need You,
need Your courage, I have
no one else to turn to
but You, You enrich our
lives with grace and pardon.
So I ask for myself,
will You take on my life,
it is under attack,
it hangs on Your response,
on no one's but Yours, no
one else can match You.
If You save me it will
earn You a world of faith
eager to speak Your name.
O God, wonderful God,
You are the miracle
I want to know, I want
to follow, You alone,
by heart, You the teacher.
My thanks will be so deep!
My sense of You so great!
The love in You is strong.
It can reach me in hell.
There is a war against me,
crude attempts at murder.

They think I am not Yours.
How unlike them You are,
sympathetic, patient
to a fault, forgiving,
faithful to an extreme.
You must stand in my place.
Let me win against them,
get my life free of them!
You do it! They will see
You and taste their own shame!
O, if it were You, if
my courage were just You!

Psalm 88

PSALM 88

You are my life,
God, over and over my life,
will You hear me
say it, will You understand it,
a living death
is all I lead, body and soul.
People treat me
already as the ghost I am.
I sprawl like a
battlefield corpse in a fresh grave,
You forget where
You buried it, You feel nothing.
You threw me here,
no light, no limit to this place,
but I feel You
raging at me, the weight of You
splitting me off
from friends; they think I am hateful.
You lock me in.
I lose sight of You in this hole.
O God, over
and over I try to reach You.
If You surprise
the dead, do they thank you for it?
Do they tell each
other below how kind You are?
How beautiful
in darkness or oblivion?
I beg You, God
to let me be Your morning praise.
Why is it You
refuse me, God, why turn Your back?

(over)

Around, around
I go the torments before death.
There is nothing
Left of me after Your fury,
Your rising tide
of it until I am alone,
nobody here
but myself and death for a friend.

Psalm 90

PSALM 90

O God, come back to us,
our hold on life is You!
Earth shapes are born in time.
Your life was never born.
Do not order us back
to the slime of the earth.
Time is nothing for You,
a night, a day, and gone.
People You cut at night
lie limp as grass by dawn.
Those You cut in daylight
lie withered by sunset.
We burn up under You.
Your anger strikes our lives.
You glare at our sins, You
blind us staring at them.
Your anger speeds up time,
makes years a single breath,
a life of seventy,
or eighty with some grace,
its pride, its pleasures, its
sins, gone in one short breath.
Who knows why You strike those
who love You so fiercely?
Tell us why You number
our days, we need that truth.
Come back, God, will You, soon?
We lead pitiful lives.
Dawn on all our days, fill
them with love and cheering
so they cancel with joy
the years of pain You caused.

Everyone should feel it,
old and young, Your power.
We ask Your loveliness
to shine on us, O God,
on our work for ourselves,
and on our work for You.

Psalm 91

PSALM 91

You that hold God
for your strength and live
in God's shadow
say, "My trust is You!"

God lures away
anyone who holds you
in a death bind,
frees you with wings that
will cover you,
will keep you for good
safe from conflict,
shielded from terror
which haunts the night,
which hunts the daytime
armed with death,
the stroke of midnight,
the stroke of noon
killing its thousands,
not killing you,
who watch crime paying
its own in kind
from God's shadow, God
who shuts out harm
from plaguing your life,

as if angels
flew guard at your feet
for stones, snakes, beasts,
to keep you hurt free.

Whoever holds
me, I will set free.

(over)

Whoever knows
me, calls me by name,
I will answer,
bad times or good times,
with gifts of life,
and show them my strength.

PSALM 93

You are
the rule, the rich cloth,
rich robe,
rich buckle of rule!
We are
the ruled, we will not
break down!
You made chaos yield
to You
for once and for good!
Chaos
reared its rip tides,
chaos
roared its thunders,
chaos
rammed its breakers!
You were
stronger than roaring,
stronger
than ramming breakers,
stronger
than howling heaven!
You are
our rule to the end!
We are
Your praise to the end!

PSALM 95

Chant your joy to God,
our rock, our safety.
Come shout and sing to
the presence of God,

more than matching idols,
ruling them all,
handling depths and heights
of ocean and peaks,
owning the sea, shaping
the earth by hand.

Come worship the Lord,
bodies bowed,
sheep to God our maker,
flock to shepherd.

Hear God speak today:

Do not stiffen
your hearts as at the Quarrel
or at the Test,
that day in the desert when
they doubted Me
though they saw My work,
your two-faced kind.

I stood them forty years,
that perverse lot.
I said, they will not have Me.
I swore in anger,
they will not reach My land.

PSALM 96

Your harmony for God
  must grow all over new
and full of God and grace,
  by name, from sea to sea,
for winning back the world!
  Let it echo God's charm
to every soul alive,
  God's displays of power!
They are great, dignified,
  awesome beyond any
ragtag pagan trifles.
  God put skies above us,
every step with tools of
  light, grandeur, and beauty!
You must, you must honor
  God, every race of you,
give God the praise the work
  of God demands, you must!
Come to God with a gift.
  At the sight of God bow
and tremble with delight!
  Then say it abroad: God
rules; the world is braced not
  to crumble; God is braced
to judge all life by truth!
  Watch the skies flush with joy,
the earth turn glad, the sea
  and its booming voices,
crag and creature, forest
  and tree, watch them explode
with their joy when God comes,
  when God comes to take hold

(over)

of the earth and rule it,
    rule it with justice, rule
it with absolute truth!

PSALM 97

God looms!
  Taste your joy, you earth,
    you fabled places!
God comes!
  In clouds massed for rain,
    firm set on a seat
      of justice and truth!
God blazes!
  Lightning back and forth,
    stroke by stroke freezing
      awe on every face!
God looks!
  Mountains melt like wax
    mastered by its flame!
God booms!
  Above, a justice
    no one can avoid!

Below,
  if you boast little
    clay gods, taste their dust!
Bow low,
  little clay, to one God!

You, God,
  You give your daughters
    and sons cause for joy!
You, God,
  You tower above
    the earth, the clay gods!
You, God,
  You love, You embrace

(over)

those who shun evil,
　　You break the grip of
　　　evil on their lives!

You bloom,
　　you lovers of God,
　　　like a planted field,
　　　　your hearts in flower!
You bloom,
　　in God, your justice,
　　　your truth. God be thanked!

Psalm 98

PSALM 98

A new song,
sing it to God
who did wonders
to make us,
wonders to show
every country
how justice
never forgets
its loyal love
for Israel.

No spot on earth
but saw God win.

Fill with joy,
make music explode
to God from harps,
from cantors,
from horn to horn,
thunder sea-worlds,
thunder lands,
clap the rivers,
cheer the mountains
like a bell,

for the presence
of the ruler
who has come
to right the world.

PSALM 100

Break out shouting
joy to God, you earth,
reach God singing
your summit of joy.

Know it is God
who made us belong
to the flock, God
who owns this people.

Chant at the door,
chant into the square
the name, Holy
God, thanks be, thanks be

to our good God
for a faithful love,
life after life,
no one can destroy.

Psalm 102

PSALM 102

I was numb with troubles
when I said this prayer:

God, listen, I ask You,
hear what I have to tell.

Look at my grief, look now,
I need a quick answer.

My life is smoke, gone fast,
my bones are burning low.
My heart is withered grass
someone crops to the roots.

I rot with complaining,
all skeleton and skin.
I look like a vulture,
I look like a famished owl.
I am a roof-sparrow
chattering and sleepless.

It is death who grabs me,
death who eats me away.

I eat soot for my food,
wash it down with my tears.

You did this, your fury
heaved me up, hurled me down.

Life thins like a shadow,
it dies like withered grass.

(over)

Your rule lasts forever,
God, Your throne always lasts.

Leave Your throne, it is time,
time to feel for Sion.
We love what's left of her,
pity her stones, her dust.

Your name will awe nations,
Your beauty touch rulers,
when You raise her rubble
and show Your loveliness,
because You heard her pray,
You did not scorn her plea.

Those who live after me
must know this to praise You:

"From the pure sky above,
God scrutinized the earth
to spot the groaning jails,
to free those set for death
so all Jerusalem
might say the name of God
when nations and rulers
come to Sion to serve."

Before You, my strength pales,
my active days are brief.

Do not take half my life
when You have life to spare!

You built this house the earth,
You built the sky by hand.
They will fall, not You,
they will be like old clothes,
You will slip out of them,
never wear them again.

But You stay who You are,
no year will be Your last.

Our children, their children,
will be safe here with You.

Psalm 103

PSALM 103

Deep down I know
I must thank God, I must
remember it is God
in every gift
Who takes away my sins,
Who brings me back to health,
Who frees me from terror
and makes my life rise up
filled with lasting beauty
like an eagle reborn.
God is the one
Who stands for all victims,
Who proved it to Moses
and our people.
We are not sins to God,
not crimes, not punishments.
God's forgiveness defeats
hell for those who believe,
puts east and west between
our rebel deeds and their due.
God feels our lives
as every parent does;
as potters know their clay,
God knows our form.
We have a life
like grass, like wild flowers.
A dry wind comes, we die,
we leave no trace.
Not so with God
Whose kindness to us lasts
life after life, a gift
for keeping faith.

(over)

God is royal
but touches all of us.
You spirits serving God
like armed forces,
you messengers
who bring us God's commands,
you peoples, places, things,
thank God, thank God!

Deep down I know
I must thank God!

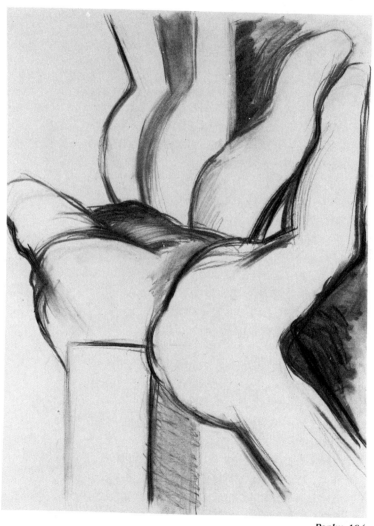

Psalm 104

PSALM 104

God, You delight my soul!

You are noble and mine,
richly clothed in beauty.
You made the sun Your coat.
You pitched the tent, the sky,
made rooms to store water,
used clouds for a roadbed,
used wings, messenger winds
and servant tongues of fire.
You built the earth firmly
so it would not collapse,
made the sea a blanket
so it covered mountains.
Then from Your thunder-voice
the water raced away,
to run hills, to find holes,
to fit in every place.
You drew lines for tides
so not to drown the land.
You sprang the torrents free
to tumble down gorges,
to water the cattle
and let the wild ass drink,
basins for all birdlife
and ponds for raucous crows.
You splash rain on the hills.
You store goods in the earth,
grow grass to feed livestock,
mow hay for the plow ox,
summon grain from the fields
and wine to fatten us,
to make us flush with health

and glow with bodily strength.
You water cedars You
planted in Lebanon,
cedars for nesting birds,
junipers for storks' nests.
You put wild goats on peaks,
badgers in cracks of rocks,
teach moons to wax and wane,
the sun where to go down.
You draw dusk, then darkness,
set wild beasts on the prowl,
lions eager for kill,
young beggars after God.
At daybreak they creep off,
they curl up in their lairs
while we walk to our fields
and hoe them until dusk.
Your deeds delight my soul!
Your genius making them,
such different creatures.
You are a sea teeming
with fish no one can count,
a shipwright, a maker
of monsters to play with.
You remain their keeper.
They want their food from you.
At feedtime, they spot you,
they eat out of your hand!
If You renege, they die,
their spirits turn to clay.
When Your genius sets out,
dead things sprout from the earth.
Your eyes can shake the ground,

(over)

Your hand make hills erupt.
I hope I sing to You,
my God, my whole life long.
If You can hear me sing,
God, You will be my joy.
I hope sins will vanish
and evil disappear.

God, You delight my soul!

PSALM 105

Alleluja!
Tell God your thanks, alleluja!
Tell the whole world!
Sing, sing to God the miracles,
revel in shouting alleluja!
You that see God,
look for the power, look for the might,
look for the presence!
How spectacular,
what God did for us, said to us!
Remember,
we come from God's choice,
Abraham, Jacob,
their God is our God,
is God for the whole world,
Who keeps alive the promise
to everyone born,
made to Abraham, sworn to Isaac,
laid out for Jacob, for Israel forever,
to give them a land,
a fat land to inherit.
They were a fistful of aliens
dragging from place to place.
No one could hurt them!
Kings were told off to save them!
These I choose, said God,
they speak My truth, leave them be!
Then the famine of God struck
every blade of their wheat.
But God used the man, Joseph,
they sold for a slave
in ankle irons, in neck chains.

(over)

Word came, God showed him
to Pharaoh, had Pharaoh
free him, make him chamberlain,
deputy ruler, teacher
to young and old.
Then starved Israel came,
starved Jacob settled there.
Our great God bred them so
they outgrew the natives.
A hatred started, cheating their lives.
Then Moses was servant,
Aaron God's choice,
to work their escape in the desert
out of Egypt.
Then God was dark ways in the dark
so no one knew why
the river ran red, killing the fish,
frogs plagued every inch,
even Pharaoh's house,
bugs and flies pestered everything,
hail fell, not rain, lightning fell,
vines withered, fig trees rotted,
terrace trees split open,
hordes of locusts, grasshoppers
blackening the sun,
ate up every blade of grass,
every ounce of food,
the ripest of them died,
the strongest.
Out of this God brought our people.
They took heavy spoils with them
but walked unbowed,

Egyptians glad to have them go,
they had caused such fear.
There was God in the cloud cover,
God in the fire at night.
There was God in the food,
meat and bread out of the sky,
water out of a rock
spilling like a desert wash,
God who kept the promise given Abraham,
God who led them singing their joy,
led them on to seize
national power and wealth
so long as they kept
the ancient law!

Alleluja!

Psalm 107

PSALM 107

We owe thanks to God for lasting graces.
People should tell the world God paid the price
for them to set them free from terror, brought
them here from the four winds; they were strangers
in the world, without room to call their own,
so hungry, so thirsty, they stood to die;
in that state they called God and God kept them alive,
marched them straight to a place they could settle.
These owe God thanks for gifts given us all,
whose aching throats, aching bellies God filled.
Even those living a hell, shackled by pain
because they defied God and scorned the law,
their wits blurred by troubles that staggered them,
in that state they called God, and God kept them alive,
stripped their gloom from them like prison chains—
these owe God thanks for gifts given us all—
smashed open hellgate's bronze and iron hold.
Their own sins sickened them, ruined their lives.
Their food was like their sin, they almost died.
in that state they called God and God kept them alive.
Word from God cured their sin, their rash was gone.
These owe God thanks for gifts given us all,
offered on an altar and sung with joy.
Those who earn their living on merchantmen
saw many acts of God far out at sea,
gale winds as if unleashed, mountainous seas
heaving them heaven high, hell deep, yelling,
reeling like falling drunks out of control,
in that state they called God and God kept them alive.
God made the winds whispers, the waves noiseless.
There was utter relief. There was home port.
These owe God thanks for gifts given us all.
These must tell their story to God's people.
God switched rivers to sand, springs to dry mud,

(over)

orchard land to salt beds, this for evil;
switched sand back to water, dry mud to springs,
brought in famished strangers to hold the place,
to plow fields, plant vineyards, bring in fat crops.
God saw to it they grew, saw to their herds,
kept them free from attack and subjection.
The God who scorned leaders gave them desert,
put strangers in their place safe as a flock.
Goodness enjoys God's deeds, evil does not.
Wisdom knows God's gifts are given us all.

Psalm 111

PSALM 111

Alleluja

I want you
who worship God
to hear why
my thanks to God
run so deep:

for great beauty
we can see
and love seeing;

for noble
light lavish as
God always;

for a past we
can feast, full
of compassion
and mercy—

God feeding the
desperate
to keep the word
given them,

God leading them
visibly
to conquer land
of their own—

for the shape of
truth, the shape
of holiness,
they breed trust
in every law,

they will last
beyond lasting,
they are made
from faithful love;

for the price
paid to free us;

for the law
made to save us;

such is God!
A fearsome name,
holy name!

And such are we!
We owe God
our deepest truth!

If we want
wisdom, God gives
us to know!

Alleluja

PSALM 112

If you love God
and holiness, your life
will be a grace.

Your family will spread
its grace to us;
your home will be fertile,

it will be rich,
its wealth and charity
will be endless.

Your death will not; the Sun
will dawn on you,
God, God gracious and just!

You are open
with us, giving, lending,
dealing fairly.

You will not fade, we will
remember you,
you are holy to us,
you are fearless
about life, you trust God
for your courage,

you hold to what you love,
no one stops you,
no one ruins your peace,

you are lavish
to us who are needy,

no end to you!
You will be glorified!

People will hate
you for this; hatred will
eat them alive.

They will be housed by Death!

PSALM 113

Alleluja

the things of God,
the name, the name,
from now until no more,
the rise of God,
the set of God,
noon above the nations,
noon above the heavens,
beauty, beauty,
unlike any,
seated high above all,
Who bends the sky
to see the earth,
Who lifts the dusty poor,
the refugee from dung,
to sit beside
the rich, Yes! with
the rich around the world,
Who gives sterility
its pregnancy,
its praise, its joy!

Alleluja

PSALM 114

Once we were slaves
   to a pitiless race.
God brought us out
   to a merciful land—
fearsome God scattering
   sea and river,
routing hills and mountains
   like sheep or goats
afraid, afraid, both sea
   and river, why,
why, both hills and mountains,
   shivering flocks?
Quiver in fear, promised land,
   the coming God
will make you have mercy!
   the God of slaves
who melted rock to quench
   our thirst, melted
flint to bubbling water!

PSALM 115

Open people's eyes,
not to us, not to us,
to Your own glory,
God, Your own dignity,
Your faithful caring,
so people cannot say
our God is nowhere!

Our God is not under
anyone's control!

Theirs are, all hand crafted,
silversmith, goldsmith,
all with mouths but are mute,
with eyes but are blind,
all with ears but are deaf,
noses, but no twitch,
all have hands without feel,
two feet, no motion,
not one can even grunt!
Like gods, like makers,
like people who trust them!

You people of God,
you priests, you followers
of God, trust our God,
trust God's powerful help!

God make our ruler
holy, and the people
and the priests, holy.
God make those who believe

holy, the great, the small.
God make our families
grow up around us,
You, God, who made holy
both heaven and earth,
who keep heaven apart
but give us the earth.
Below the ground the dead
have nothing to say.
We, the living, bless You!
We will never stop!

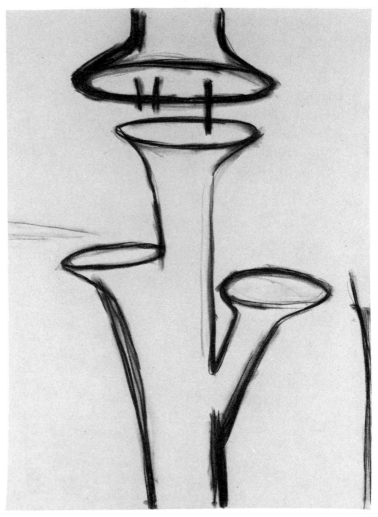

Psalm 116

PSALM 116

God's love for me
saved my life even as
    I asked for grace.
Death was a mob from hell
    out after me.
Despair took hold of me,
    so I pleaded:
God, will you get me free!
    The grace there is
to God, the compassion!
    God kept me from
the corruption of death!

I can sleep now
without fear, in God's grace.
    My life is free
of death, my eyes will not
    run with its tears,
nor my feet track its wastes.
    The fields I walk
will hold the life of God.
    I kept my faith
though death mobbed after me,
    my fearful thought:
everyone will fail you!

How can I give
to God what God gives me!
    This cup of life,
I will bless it for God;
    my promises,
I will keep them for God.

(over)

The time of death
for those who keep their faith
    is dear to God.
O God, I do serve You,
    I do keep faith.
Untie this death from me!
    My sacrifice
will be thanksgiving,
    the name I call
upon it will be Yours!

    The promises
I keep will take place here
    for all to see,
in God's household, in God's
    Jerusalem!

Alleluja

PSALM 117

You, of other peoples,
you, of other spirits,
you can cherish our God!

Our God cares mightily,
our God lives faithfully,
forever, for each one!

PSALM 121

The mountain I see,
   will it give me strength
that comes straight from God,
   maker of this world?
No one will turn back
   into mud as God sleeps,
God is beyond sleep,
   on watch over us,
a guard, a shadow,
   a force alongside.
No sun will strike us,
   no moon strike us down.
God will stop evil
   attacking our lives.
God will loom above
   our back and forth ways
for now and for good!

PSALM 122

The joy in me!
People saying to me,
  "We go in now,
we go in to God's house!"
  I stood with them
inside Jerusalem,
  inside its gates,
God's city, thick with God's
  work and working,
thick with God's pilgrims
  up to obey.
The law is, give God thanks
  in the place where
kings and judges held seats.
  They should pray peace
for you, those who love you,
  Jerusalem,
their lives should grow in you!
  Inside your walls,
peace, below your towers,
  a teeming life!
I speak for my kindred
  and friends, I pray
from my heart, be at peace!
  You hold God's house.
If I could give you peace!

PSALM 123

My eyes
will stay on You
who rule us from
above,
the eyes
of a slaveboy
on his master
for things,
the eyes
of a slavegirl
on her mistress
for things.
Our eyes
are so on You,
our God, until
You know
we need
from You relief,
O God, master,
mistress,
relief!
We are glutted
with mockery,
force fed
too long
on mockery,
from the reckless,
the proud!

Psalm 126

PSALM 126

When God gave us
our future back,
we grew like sand
out of the sea.
With laughing mouths,
runaway tongues,
we filled our lives!
We overheard
our neighbors say:
A mighty God
did show in us,
did work our joy!
Like torrents in
the desert, God
made us alive!
we were grim when
we sowed, we were
grinning reaping—
grimly out with
pouches of seed,
grinning home with
shouldering sheaves!

Psalm 128

PSALM 128

For a man
who loves, who follows God,
it is bliss

to eat food his hands grow,
in peace, in happiness,
to see his woman make
their home a fruitful vine,
to see his children crowd
at meals like olive shoots—
a vision, lasting, from God,
for a man
who loves, who follows God!

Let it be,
for you, from Sion's God,
bliss, from Jerusalem,
lifelong bliss,
from your childrens' children,
lifelong bliss,
and peace from God above!

PSALM 130

I am empty.
I raise an empty voice,
God, God, listen,
I ask You for mercy,
not for judgment,
who could stand Your judgment?
You forgive me.
I stand in awe of You.
O Israel,
my empty soul calls God,
then waits hour after hour for
its sun to rise.
Wait with me, Israel.
We will be full
of God's saving graces.
Israel, God
will heal the harm we do.

PSALM 131

God,
my soul is not
above You,
looking past You,
to trifle
with important things,
or fill itself
with thoughts beyond
its power.
My soul is calm
and quiet
waiting for You,
as a child is
with its mother,
my soul
the child with You.

My people,
wait so for God,
from now
until forever!

PSALM 133

It thrills you
to see peoples ranged
together
like lovely mountains;

it blesses,

like a fragrance poured
on Aron's
brow, and down his face,
down over
his collar and flanks;

like a dew
from Hermon drifting
south to the
ranges of Sion;

Sion where
God rains eternal
life on you!

PSALM 134

Come, grace God,
  you earth God made!
You people
  who watch in God's
  house the whole night,
come, grace God!
  Lift your prayer from
  earth to heaven!

God grace you!
  Who made you both,
  heaven and earth!

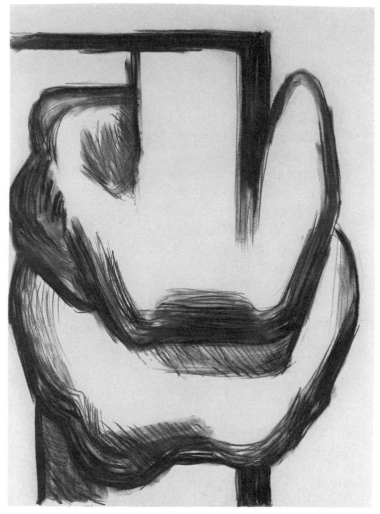

Psalm 142

PSALM 142

I pray, I pray God,
  I pray God to help me!
God must know, God must
  know this agony:

my breath is struggling,
  leaving for You know where,
You know on which road,
  a death trap every step!
Look at it lined with
  no one who knows my name,
not a soul who cares,
  escape is no escape!
Except You, You are
  my one escape, my route
to the land of life.
  O God, listen, I am
near bottom, Great God,
  free me, I am no match
for death when it hunts;
  spring me from its prison,
so I can thank You,
  in a circle of souls
You freed, O God, that
  You gave me my life back!

Psalm 143

PSALM 143

God, when I pray
for Your mercy, I fear
You will not bend.
I appeal to Your heart.
I could never
face Your justice, nor could
anyone living.
The fear of death grinds me
into the ground,
darkens my soul so I
live like the damned,
someone who has no hope,
no taste for life.
I know You made this world
with Your own hands.
I know Your works by heart.
My hands are out
empty; I thirst for You,
away from You,
my throat is dry with death.

God, I beg You,
answer soon, my life fails.
If you turn me
down, the dead will claim me.
Be dawn for me,
be the love I trusted.
Let me travel
the road of prayer to You.
Save me from death,
God, it overwhelms me.
I want to know

from You what I should do.
God, lead me to
open spaces Yourself.
I use Your name
to ask You for my life,
to save it from
those who want it destroyed.
Make death and death-
dealers nothing for me.

Psalm 145

PSALM 145

Every day forever,
God my Rule,
I will heap praise on You,
bless Your name,
praise Your name,
every day forever.

Matchless, limitless God
beyond praise,
life to life we pass down
what You made,
what You did,
to spread Your name abroad.

They say Your beauty glows.
I say You work marvels.
They say You bring on fear.
I call You heroic.
They say good to a fault,
Your justice makes them sing.

God is grace and mercy,
not anger,
lovely, good to each one
every way.

Creation praise You, God,
those with faith
bless You, glory in You,
have You known
far and wide,
what You made, what You did,
Your brilliance,

(over)

Your rule of
all times life after life.

Faithful God, gracious God,
word and deed,
God who lifts those who fall,
those who bend.

Animals look to You
at feedtime.
You nourish the living
with open hand.

Every way, every time,
God is just.
God is near those who call
from their hearts.

They have what they desire.
God hears them and saves them.

Those who love, God protects.
Those who hate, God destroys.

All flesh and I should praise
and bless God's holy name
every day forever.

PSALM 146

My soul, my body,
  my being until death,
wants to honor God
  with songs that tell the truth!
You cannot trust your
  soul to mortal rulers.
Once dead, they decay,
  your future putrefies!
You will love on if
  you trust the rule of God.
God made land, sea and
  sky and all their beings,
God, the law for the
  wronged, the voice for the crushed,
the food for the starved!
  God unlocks our prison—
unseals our blind eyes,
  unbends our crooked backs—,
God, the lover of
  the good, of the stranger,
the strength of orphans
  and widows, God the force
subverting tyrants!
  God, the rule forever!
Your God, O Sion,
  from life to life to life!

PSALM 147-A

ALLELUJA

How good and glad we are
    to sing about our God,
here, in Jerusalem!
    God rebuilt it, God called
its scattered victims back.
    God healed each broken heart,
healed each wounded body—
    Who gave each star its count
and all of them a name!
    Power beyond power,
skill beyond skill unknown,
    God, who calms small souls,
and threatens wicked ones!
    Sing to God, play to God,
your lyrical thanks be!
    God collects empty clouds,
readies them to hold rain,
    then dots the hills with grass,
gives livestock their fodder,
    and pickings to the crows!
Animal grace, human
    grace, neither can sway God.
What sways is deep respect!
    Deep attachment sways God!

PSALM 147-B

You, Jerusalem, you,
    Sion, look up! Applaud!
You are safe! God doubled
    your locks, doubled your births,
freed you from war, fed you
    full with the fattest wheat!
God speaks in licks of light,
    bellows at the mountains,
fleeces snow to scatter,
    frost to sow like ashes,
flings crumbs of hail so cold
    no one can stand the sting,
then shifts from freeze to thaw
    with wet and melting winds!
Such a God speaks to you
    in law and living rule!
To no one else! God speaks
    commands to no one else!

ALLELUJA

Psalm 148

PSALM 148

You are lovely, God!
From the pitch of the
sky they must tell You:
the angels, squads of
angels, must tell You,
sun, moon, stars of the
morning must tell You,
the rain overhead
in store must tell You,
You are lovely, God!
All loveliness comes
from Your decision!
You made it to stay
where You ordered it,
never to pass away!
From the pitch of the
deeps they must tell You,
sea monsters and all!
The fire here, the smoke,
the hail, the snow, the wind
storming to obey,
mountain top, hill top,
orchard tree, cedar tree,
beast, savage with tame,
crawler with flyer,
prince with pauper,
boy with girl with man
with woman, young, old,
must tell You, must tell
You Your lovely name!
Beyond all names made!
Lovely beyond light

(over)

of the earth or sky!
   But lavish to us,
the least of peoples!
   We live life for You!
We carry Your name!
   We tell You as well
how lovely You are!

Psalm 150

PSALM 150

To You,
to You above,
to You above holy
and strong,
be joy,
be joy from us
for boundless lifegiving
power,
joy from
our trumpets, joy
from our lyrical strings,
joy from
our drums
and dances and
harps, pipes, and shivering
cymbals,
joy from
our clashing, our
ringing with all that lives
to You!

ESSAYS

Psalm Translation: Creating a New Poem

I was asked to make English poems out of psalms. Those who asked me are convinced that most translations in contemporary English are not poetic enough. They think that if a contemporary poet/theologian is given a basic translation of a literal character, he or she—myself in this case—will be able to recover the psalm through a new act of poetic creation. The new poem is to work in a paradoxical way, its quality as an artwork in contemporary English will provide the spiritual experience of relationship with God which the original artwork intended, though the new poem is related to the old as art to art, not as mirror to face. Another purpose is to be served: the new poem made of the old one will create a further spiritual experience by expanding the scope of the original to include the contemporary without violating the integrity of either. It is a contemporary person who uses psalms as the expression of his or her soul to God or as the voice of God back. It is also a contemporary liturgist, composer, preacher, lector, who will be conditioned by a creative translation. Different styles provoke different responses because styles are metaphors in their own right. The people who want the poetry of psalms intensified in English clearly believe that the aesthetic experience is the spiritual experience. They do not accept a separation between an expression and an experience. They want the unity restored so that it is the psalm which provides the relationship to God, world and self, not the occasion of the psalm.[1]

I agreed to try doing what people asked me as a poet and a theologian.[2] What moved me to accept was the belief I also have that the aesthetic beauty of certain religious expressions is the truth of those expressions. Now, sometime later, I have been asked to say what consciousness I have come to about recreating psalms into modern poems so that I might serve as a case study in success or failure for those who are convinced that the beauty of a psalm is the source of its spiritual meaning, and therefore the beauty of a translation is the one way to make a psalm's spiritual truth available to a community of belief. Understand the word beauty to

[1] ICEL, Brief On The Liturgical Psalter, *Pilot Study On A Liturgical Psalter* (Feb. 1982) 7-12.

[2] F. Sullivan, Poetic Psalms, *The Bible Today* (March 1981) 121-126.

mean what several traditions say it means, a charming material, like a human face, which creates its own space, draws us into communion with its own transcendence, and looks back at us for our good and our freedom.[3] The charism of beauty is its ability to create freedom in relationship, and to refuse owning or being owned, as in idolatries.[4] The relationship is iconic, as in Rublev's *Holy Trinity*, or in Chagall's *White Crucifixion*, or in Orozco's *El Hombre de Fuego*.

Halfway through my project, I know I can do about eighty psalms of the one hundred and fifty. These eighty engage my imagination sympathetically so that I want to make them modern English poems.[5] Some among them have great lyric play, some remarkable narrative intensity, some are profoundly confessional or didactic through imagery, some have feeling levels that are intricate and dignified in every human sense: they have a taste for a creating God, redeeming God, which is strong and lasting. The psalms I cannot approach are the ones that make my imagination powerless. Some require of the beauty of God or of the earth that they serve to destroy that which is against God or the earth. Some manifest the ugliness of revenge, the ugliness of cursing, some the narrowness of bigotry, some are exercises in hatred or exclusiveness.

These latter render my imagination powerless poetically and theologically because I work as a lyric poet and I have to feel at one with what I say. I cannot simply provide a source of language for feelings I cannot live without ruining my aesthetic hope. I have tried; I sense the loss, or I have it pointed out to me. I also work as a theologian who sees God as creator and redeemer, not destroyer and damner. I do not believe what I say if I translate lines claiming that God causes this or that slaughter for this or that

---

[3]Cf. J.-P. Manigne, *Pour Une Poétique De La Foi,* Paris 1969, 45. Also, H.-G. Gadamer, *Truth And Method,* London 1975, 345-447.
[4]Cf. H. Marcuse, *The Aesthetic Dimension,* Boston 1978, III & V. Also, G. Durand, *L'Imagination Symbolique,* Paris 1968, 34-35.
[5]I am deeply influenced in this by Burton Raffel, *The Forked Tongue. A Study Of The Translation Process,* The Hague 1971, 11-23, 163-176, & 160: "The challenge to me, as translator and poet, is to make—to discover really—an englished incarnation which I can then possess without diminution."

good reason. Again, I have tried; I sense my insincerity, or I have it pointed out to me. I think that a lyric imagination has to be like the Suffering Servant of Isaiah's songs, willing to transform destruction into creation if at all possible, or like the poet of Job who refuses to permit God or Job to curse each other and die.

Those psalms that celebrate creation and redemption almost ask of themselves to become modern poems. The modern lyric in English has had to face so much destruction and damnation in history that it chooses every means possible to counteract that history. I do not mean escapism. I mean the lyric's refusal to take part in destruction and damnation, its attempt to humanize the destroyers and to manifest a transcendence much like the transcendence of the Suffering Servant. Such psalms also ask to become part of modern theology. These days, theology can only handle the God of compassion and make sense. The God who causes or permits evil in order to produce good ruins belief especially in innocent victims and in those who absorb the experience of innocent victims into their own. Psalms that beg compassion or speak compassionately blend into modern consciousness readily and do not split the one who uses them into a Dr. Jekyll and Mr. Hyde.

There are mixed psalms, creative and redemptive in the beginning, destructive and damnational at the end. The lyric imagination works with wholes, its treatment of the finish of a psalm conditions its treatment of the start. A lyric imagination at work on translation sees where it is going with its first words, rhythms, images. Theological understanding is also anticipatory, it knows starts and finishes, often with the same immediacy as imagination. For my imagination, my mind, mixed type psalms are very difficult to handle, and I either have to transpose the damnational passages into allegory or not touch the whole psalm. I am describing what happens, not what I wish to happen. To repeat, my schooling in the modern lyric in English and in modern theologies of the compassionate God make me trust the qualities of some psalms and mistrust the qualities of others. A different sort of imagination, a more dramatic one, might not experience the same divisions I do. The lyric imagination is not above the human condition. It is not the one innocent among the many guilty. It is more like a prayer for restoration for all the broken forms, coming from an accomplice in the breaking who wishes to be so no more. Here is

154

my version of Psalm 88:

> You are my life,
> God, over and over my life,
> will you hear me
> say it, will you understand it,
> a living death
> is all I lead, body and soul.
> People treat me
> already as the ghost I am.
> I sprawl like a
> battlefield corpse in a fresh grave,
> you forget where
> you buried it, you feel nothing.
> You threw me here,
> no light, no limit to this place,
> but I feel you
> raging at me, the weight of you
> splitting me off
> from friends; they think I am hateful.
> You lock me in.
> I lose sight of you in this hole.
> O God, over
> and over I try to reach you.
> If you surprise
> the dead, do they thank you for it?
> Do they tell each
> other below how kind you are?
> How beautiful
> in darkness or oblivion?
> I beg you, God,
> to let me be your morning praise.
> Why is it you
> refuse me, God, why turn your back?
> Around, around
> I go the torments before death.
> There is nothing
> left of me after your fury,
> your rising tide
> of it until I am alone,
> nobody here
> but myself and death for a friend.

I used Dahood's Anchor Bible translation as the basis for my poetic/theological decisions. Though Dahood's English is poor, his sense of the poetic is rich; he uncovers imagery well and consistently. This psalm requires a sense of immediacy because death threatens the relationship. Immediacy requires direct address, compression, insistance, repeatedly. The image underlying all the language is that of the grave. It is an image kindred to "Sheol" in the older translations, and to "living burial" in descriptions of modern camps—concentration or gulag. It is kindred to the image of jail and of human plight in the ancient and modern senses. The image does three things at once: it works as itself in the psalm version; it echoes the traditional imagery of the underworld; it echoes the imagery of modern victims. I think it does this triple work modestly, i.e., the psalm does not conquer other experiences for itself, nor does it pretend to be a "holier than thou" religious expression. Far greater suffering has been recorded in far greater poetry. There are split emotions throughout the psalm which result from the contradictory relationship: the God of life is seen as the God of death, the God of love as the God of hatred. The psalmist begs life and love from the source of death and hatred, hoping to argue that source back to lifegiving and loving. All the images conspire to return the relationship to one of life and love. A short stammering style derives from the images and the feelings they express. I use a syllable count to each line, 4/8/4/8 throughout, letting the accent float, so there could be a dialectic of order/disorder on the sound level, and so there could be for readers and composers both an expectedness and unexpectedness to the lines. The words themselves are kept to as straight a sentence structure as possible, to mirror the undeviating intensity of focus and repetition in the psalmist's consciousness. The basic tone is one of powerful longing, longing for a relationship of love and life, not for pure safety apart and untouchable by anyone. There is some bitterness, some anger playing through nearly all the lines, even some gallows humor. These elements do not overbear the basic tone. The psalm is through-composed in my version so the whole of it has to be used. Excerpting lines will be a rupture of the psalm's integrity.[6] Here

[6]For an excellent study of poetic structures, as structures, and their power to intimate transcendent meaning, cf. J.G. Lawler, *Celestial Pantomime: Poetic Structures of Transcendence,* New Haven 1979.

is my version of Psalm 104:

God, you delight my soul!

You are noble and mine,
richly clothed in beauty
You made the sun your coat.
You pitched the tent, the sky,
made rooms to store water,
used clouds for a roadbed,
used wings, messenger winds
and servant tongues of fire.
You built the earth firmly
so it would not collapse,
made the sea a blanket
so it covered mountains.
Then from your thunder-voice
the water raced away,
to run hills, to find holes,
to fit in every place.
You drew lines for tides
so not to drown the land.
You sprang the torrents free
to tumble down gorges,
to water the cattle
and let the wild ass drink,
basins for all birdlife
and caucus ponds for crows.
You splash rain on the hills.
You store goods in the earth,
grow grass to feed livestock,
mow hay for the plow ox,
summon grain from the fields
and wine to fatten us,
to make us flush with health
and glow with bodily strength.
You water cedars you
planted in Lebanon,
cedars for nesting birds,
junipers for storks' nests.
You put wild goats on peaks,
badgers in cracks of rocks,
teach moons to wax and wane,

the sun where to go down.
You draw dusk, then darkness,
set wild beasts on the prowl,
lions eager for kill,
young beggars after God.
At daybreak they creep off,
they curl up in their lairs
while we walk to our fields
and hoe them until dusk.
Your deeds delight my soul!
Your genius making them,
such different creatures.
You are a sea teeming
with fish no one can count,
a shipwright, a maker
of monsters to play with.
You remain their keeper.
They want their food from you.
At feedtime they spot you,
they eat out of your hand!
If you renege, they die,
their spirits turn to clay.
When your genius sets out,
dead things sprout from the earth.
Your eyes can shake the ground,
your hand make hills erupt.
I hope I sing to you,
my God, my whole life long.
If you can hear me sing,
God, you will be my joy.
I hope sins will vanish
and evil disappear.

    God, you delight my soul!

   I think the psalm has to be done as a breathless narrative which shows its delight in God through its delight in language and imagery of the most sweeping kind. The psalmist becomes God, in fact, in order to see the exuberance of God at work in sustaining creation. So a reader or composer can grasp the exuberance of God only in the psalmist's prodigal narrative and imagery. The line structure is to a syllable count 6/6 throughout, again to give a substructure to the careening narrative. There are many lines which simply run over, one into the other. There are also lines which are short explosions of wonder. Both types of lines together create a sense of chaos and order in constant dialectic, and a sense that the divine creation works with the same dialetic as the physical elements of the poem. The act of poetic creation is the metaphor for the act of world creation, the ecstasy of the one reveals the ecstasy of the other. This psalm also must be used whole. I have shifted the destructive elements toward the end from the concrete to the abstract, hoping that the shift will retain some sense of the destructive wish while retaining also the creative bearing of the whole psalm. Otherwise those elements rip the whole poem apart. Here is my version of Psalm 6:

> You are angry at me.
> You punish me.
> Please stop, I am worn out.
> Stand in my place.
> I am hurt to the bone,
> my soul a bruise.
> Will you keep after me?
> Change, please, cure me,
> save me, you are not harsh.
> Can a dead mouth
> know what to sing for praise?
> I cry myself
> to sleep, no song, so tired,
> my pillow damp.
> I darken what I see,
> deaden my heart.
> I know my tears reach you.
> Death has no hold.
> You take these words from me.
> You accept me.
> You shake death loose from me.
> You bury it.

I decided to let nothing disperse the intensity of the psalmist speaking to God without blinking or looking aside. I do not even spare the time to say God, the 'you' repeated is direct, first as a recognition of the one who is the source of the pain, then of the one who can take the pain away, then of the one who can listen to how bad the psalmist feels, then of the one who lifts the burden

159

that caused the pain at the start. The relationship is unbroken throughout; it shifts as music shifts without pause from heaviness to lightness. God is revealed in the varying 'you' of the lines, especially in the last four where relief and love mount in the firm, declarative sentences. The last sentences are the reverse in feeling of the first two, though they have the same declarative structure. The verse lines again are set to a syllable count, 6/4 throughout, yet there is a constant interruption within the lines to show the struggle of the psalmist to figure out what is to come of this life and death crisis. I have understood the final lines in an allegorical sense to mean the same death that threatens in the earlier part of the poem. This way I can keep a consistency of imagery through the poem and use the image, at the end, as a reversal of itself.

In the last example I will use, I failed badly. It is the Samekh section of Psalm 119:

I hate fickle minds; I choose to love your law.
You defend me, you command me, I wait on you.
Clear off, you scum, and let me obey my God.
Shore up my life, you promised, or you shame my hope.
God, keep me on my feet so I respect your word.
Bury all renegades; they adore what is false.
You treat evil as scum, so I love your law.
My skin crawls in awe and fear at the way you judge.

Burton Raffel wrote me about it, "This is perhaps the worst of the sequence—and when a poet of your calibre falls this flat . . . it's got to be what in law is called 'a flaw in the inception.'" He goes on to say, "It's not the poet who so thinks, but someone else, some other part of you, maybe the theological side, maybe the public-priest side, I don't know. But I do know it's not the poet part of Francis Sullivan." Raffel is my touchstone in all this work of making English language poems of psalms. My imagination simply did not connect with this love-of-the-law psalm. I was not able to find an image in myself which would reveal the image of the law. The translation is therefore mainly a display of verbal facility which is neither poetry nor theology. It may be that the psalm itself is a headstrong thing in the original and refuses poetic treatment. When the aesthetic basis is right, the poem is germinated from within its own means and it reveals its own spirituality. When the aesthetic basis is wrong, the work is germinated from outside itself and turns into propaganda. I have to say that several priests and theologians did praise this which I am calling a poetic failure. I do not want to call them or myself and Raffel into question. I want only to bring out again two difficulties a poet-translator of psalms must face: he or she must create a work of art out of material that piety and liturgical use consider sacred whether it is artistically presented or not: he or she must find critics who know when the aesthetic basis and the piety are one in the work and when they are not. People can use this failed poetic translation because they can bring to it what it does not seem to have. We all must do this with many different texts.[7] I began this essay by citing the problem that we must use translations of poetic texts that do not manifest well the nature of the original through the nature of the translation, and therefore we lose something essential from the original experience.[8] I am speaking of contemporary translations used in liturgical settings, not about translations, transformations, done by poets in original ways, which are attempts to revive the psalm tradition, used or not in liturgical assemblies.[9] I can conclude with a series of statements about the problem I was asked to resolve as a poet and theologian.

An act of creation presented to a community gives it an experience of spiritual freedom. Poetic creation is one way. It reveals a primary activity of God and a primary activity of humankind, as we believe in both. Poetic translations make privileged texts available in a new language as acts of creation. The aesthetic beauty of the translation shows a community that the spiritual truth it believes in occurs equally within its own tongue. Its own tongue is not a conqueror. It is a mate. This realization gives to the community a chance to enter into an adult union with God, not an adolescent union fitfully obedient and disobedient. The union is one of eros. The charm of the medium, the poetic text, is erotic charm because it asks the whole of a self to give and receive a whole self, and yet the poetic text insists on retaining the dif-

[7]H. Gardner, *Religion And Literature,* New York 1971, 131 re: traditional religious forms which go beyond judgments about quality.

[8]Cf. Peter Levi, *The English Bible 1534-1859,* Grand Rapids 1974, 9-41.

[9]Cf. D. Rosenberg, *Blues Of The Sky,* New York 1976, 47-53. D. Berrigan, *Uncommon Prayer. A Book Of Psalms.* New York. 1978.

ference between one beloved and another.[10] The poetic translation is not the poetic original. And yet they are mates in belief, in loss of faith, in recovery, in penitence, in desperate hope, in lyric ecstasy, in the love of creation and redemption.

Failure to renew an act of creation by another act leads to an experience of subjection in a community.[11] Union with God becomes one sided, non-erotic; it becomes extrinsic, and beauty becomes an idol to distract the soul from its emptiness toward God, beauty becomes the image of the split from God, the place of the satanic, not the image of transcendence and the defeat of isolation. The lesson is not learned that the poetry of revelation, in its original, in its translation, gets free of ownership, free of propaganda, free of sectarianism, free of institution, and serves thereby as a reminder that humankind is free in the face of God, and God is free in the face of humankind, so that the relationship between the two must be created all the time, never coerced. How both God and humankind treat the medium of relationship, the psalm in this instance, the psalm translation, has everything to do with their integrity. Psalms that beg God to destroy and damn the sinful are a rape of poetry, and therefore a rape of relationship. Psalms that order humankind to destroy in God's name are equally a rape of relationship. The psalmist has control of both human and divine voice. The translator comes next. Then the community which lives what it expresses, or tries to, though often it lives around what it expresses, praying a violence, living a peacefulness.

I sense that people who want poetic translations of poetic originals, psalms, have a definite spirituality in mind. They want a love of integrity of form. Integrity of form means that beauty cannot be lost without the loss of truth. The truth is creative and redemptive. It is not destructive by intent, nor is it damnational. The passion, death, and resurrection of any form reveals over and over the nature of God living with the nature of humankind. Liturgy is a medium of that living. Liturgy which does not respect the integrity of its material disjoints the living. Liturgy which does, creates a chance for love anyone can choose.

[10]Cf. P. Evdokimov, *L'Art De L'Icône: Théologie De La Beauté*, Paris 1972, 199. What is said there of the icon refers also to the psalm-poem.
[11]D. Sölle, *Imagination Et Obéissance*, Paris 1970.

162

Spiritual Imagery: Some Rules

There is a spirituality to living by the imagination, in or out of religion—the classical points of reference are all involved: 1) someone relates to someone or to something in a life-giving or a death-dealing way, and is open to life-giving or death-dealing at the same time; 2) the means of life or death must be invented continually, or adjusted, or abandoned; 3) the wish is to arrive at a lasting union or lasting separation.[1] Imagination is the power to do this, to invent, to adjust, or to abandon the means and therefore the relationship. I want to try to illustrate rather than argue what I mean. The argument has been well made many times.[2] The experience of creating or recreating beauty will serve my purpose best because it breeds a sense of "sacramental relationship which lasts always.[3] The opposite experience of destroying or conspiring in the destruction of beauty breeds a sense of permanent cleavage. I know only the verbal arts, poetry especially, so I can only hope to make sense to those who practice or entertain the other arts.

Take Psalm 29 in Dahood's translation.[4] It is a thunder storm lyric borrowed nearly word for word from a Canaanite original. The Hebrew borrower put his own verses at either end of the poem, and in the body of it, the storm, wrote in Jahweh for Baal. The poem in its original imitates, by means of its phonetic and narrative sweep, the progress of a storm in from the Mediterranean, over the coast of Palestine to the forests, the mountains, to, voila!, a vision of Jahweh enthroned for a chosen people in the one Temple at Jerusalem forever! Dahood uses a traditional Bible English to catch the storm with words and does it well inside that vocabulary. And we read it—as a lyric, or as a sacred text never mind the lyric, or as a personal and communal prayer/meditation

[1]Cf. André Ravier, ed. *La Mystique Et Les Mystiques* (Paris Desclée De Brouwer, 1965).

[2]Cf. William F. Lynch, *Christ And Prometheus* (Notre Dame: Notre Dame University Press, 1970). *Images of Faith* (Notre Dame: Notre Dame University Press, 1973).

[3]The phrase is Kenneth Rexroth's.

[4]Mitchell Dahood, *Psalms 1-50* (Garden City: Doubleday & Co., 1966), pp. 174-180.

text. We also read it as a "lying word"[5]—as a seduction, or as a terrible misuse of an aesthetic experience, the propagandizing of nature.

Suppose we read it just for the beauty of the image, a storm in words, whether the storm means Baal or Jahweh or nature, for the lyric poet of it, or lyric editor, or translator, playing creation's own game, managing chaos and its meaning from some imaginative "on high."

A Psalm Of David

Give Yahweh, O gods,
   give Yahweh glory and praise,
Give Yahweh the glory due his name!
Bow down to Yahweh
   when the Holy One appears.
The voice of Jahweh
   is upon the waters,
The God of glory
   rolls the thunder;
Yahweh is upon the mighty waters.
The voice of Jahweh
   is strength itself,
The voice of Jahweh
   is very splendor.
The voice of Jahweh
   shivers the cedars,
And Jahweh
   shivers the cedars of Lebanon;
The voice of Jahweh
   cleaves with shafts of fire.
He makes Lebanon skip like a calf,
   and Sirion like a young wild ox.
The voice of Jahweh
   convulses the steppe,
Yahweh convulses
   the steppe of Kadesh.
The voice of Jahweh
   makes the hinds writhe

[5]The phrase is Laura Riding Jackson's.

164

And strips the forests bare;
While in his temple—all of it,
   a vision of the Glorious One.
Yahweh has sat enthroned
   from the flood,
And Yahweh has sat enthroned,
   the king from eternity.
Yahweh will give his people victory,
   Yahweh will bless his people with peace.

There are the rival gods, now edited into angels, instructed how to behave before the One God. There is the storm, Jahweh, lead across the landscape. There is the landscape writhing in labor. There is the lightning flashing its vision down on a holy place. There is the calm, the soothing aftermath of the storm-God over the one land. There is the taste of peace. Someone imagined this scenario through a great play of words, someone else stole it and added to it, someone else translated it into imitative English.

The sense of God that is created through the sense of the storm is intense. But the storm is the meaning of the psalm, the one the psalmist has created in order to relate to God, to the earth, to what happens in the play between God and the earth. The psalmist knows that God is not the storm, that the storm is its own power and destructiveness and peaceful aftermath.[6] Yet it breeds a sense of what it takes to create by overcoming chaos with order. And that is God. It breeds a sense of earth-shaking beauty—color, sound, expanse, motion, wind and water, a thrilling, fearful beauty. And that is God, a thrilling, fearful beauty. It breeds a sense of aftermath, the repair of ruin by peace. And that is God. Without the storm of words, there is no knowledge of the storm of God against chaos, against the recalcitrant earth, against idolatry, in order to bring a vision of lasting life to prevail. The psalmist, the translator, created the storm, created the sense of God in the storm, accepted the creation as true, and believed about God what the storm taught. The relationship is life-giving. The psalmist has been brought to create something beautiful as a means of responding to someone without turning the means into a lie about itself, or

[6]Mircea Eliade, *The Sacred And The Profane* (New York: Harcourt, Brace, 1959).

about God, or about the psalmist. I think the psalm has the beauty
of a collage. It is clear what has been borrowed. It is clear what
has been added. I get the sense that all who were involved in
working on it loved the beauty of the storm, the storm language,
and the sense of the sacred the storm seemed to reveal. That love
saves the collage-work for me, though I wish I had the original
poem with its original Baal.

Allow me to take that love of beauty in the original poet, in the
psalmist, in the translator, one step further, into my own love of
the beauty of the storm and of its language, and do a further
reworking, using techniques of contemporary poetry to bring out
what I think is missing in Dahood's version, a sense of vivid immediacy, a sense of through-composition, a sense of play.

> Applaud,
> little gods, applaud
> your God,
> you owe your glory!
> Bow low
> when The Holy looms,
> the voice
> looms in from the sea,
> God, God,
> booming in thunder,
> God, loose,
> out, over the deep,
> strong voice,
> power itself, bright
> voice, light
> itself, loose from God,
> splitting
> cedars to splinters,
> cedars
> of Lebanon, God's sharp
> blows are
> licks of fire, down, down,
> they bounce
> the earth, bounce the hills
> like beasts,
> wild, skipping oxen.
> Thunder!
> God buckles the fields.

Thunder!
God labors the deer
and bares
the forests of leaves.
Thunder!
God's temple flares up,
flares with
visions of glory!
The throne
of God since chaos,
the throne
of God forever!
God, God,
maker of triumph,
God, God,
of chaos and peace!

The spirituality of the psalm can be sketched now as follows: God is the awesome beauty of order locked in struggle with the awesome terror of chaos so as to overcome chaos and bring a lasting life to those who see the struggle and long for order to win out. The act of creating the psalm, or recreating it, teaches this: the psalmist, the reworkers, the translators, the readers, have had to struggle with experience, with language, with form, to get even a glimpse of this truth, have had to undergo chaos to find the order, have had to sense that life flows back and forth between themselves and God because of the lyric's beauty. The meaning of the storm is freely chosen. There are many other interpretations possible at the same time. Some are kindred, some are not: God is both creation and destruction; God is a mindless force; nature is chance good, chance evil; nature is sexual conflict, a passion that rapes in order to start life, a passion that undergoes rape in order to bear life. No interpretation is forced on the imagination. Yet the storm yields up these meanings, it is not like a rorschach blot having nothing to do with what one sees in it. The lyric creates its truth from the truth of the storm: the struggle to create reveals the love of God for the earth, the love of the earth for God; it reveals the risk of destructiveness they both undergo in relating to one another this way, as well as the risk of a lasting union, a scene of freshness and peace.

Some half-dozen psalms use the image of storm or weather as the icon of relationship with God. The relationships are varied. Psalm

72 says the soul must remember God "from a bleak gorge, a trap-ped/place, from mountains ringed around it,/echoes top to bottom,/strokes of thunder, lightning, rolling/waves breaking overhead. . .⁷" Psalm 65 exults in the power God's rain has to dress the earth like a bride; "Shiver the stars of dawn/and dusk with joy./Come, make a laughing earth,/thicken her trees,/fill the sky wells with water,/rain wheat on her,/you made her to bear crops!/Make her sopping,/ridge and furrow, shower/her with fresh buds,/crown her peaks with rain,/thicken her grass,/fat grass that never ends,/ribbon her hills,/dress her hollows in flocks,/shawl her valleys,/wheat for the jubilee!" Psalm 74 puts it up to God who conquered chaos in primordial times to conquer evil in historical times. There is almost a frenzy in the lines: "Why not defeat/them, God, here, in this place?/You fought the sea, you smashed its waves rearing/their fearsome heads./You fed sea monsters to the desert tribes./You made water of sand,/sand of water,/switching them back and forth." Then in Psalm 77, equally a frenzied psalm, there is another pagan lyric borrowed for the psalmist's purposes, to beg God to exert in a personal situation a power God exerted at the origin of the world: "There was a time/when chaotic forces,/like floods loose,/shook in fear when they saw/you come at them,/your massed clouds pelting rain,/your voice booming/light zigzag cloud to cloud,/thunder ringing/the sky, lightning stripp-ing/night from the earth,/shaking it to its roots./You struck a path/through those forces like rain/drubbing the sea,/then leaving not a trace/of your fury/for anyone to see." Psalm 93 is kindred to psalm 29, God is the victory of creative over destructive forces, thus God wins life for us. The same is true of psalm 97. In psalm 147, the psalmist says: "God speaks in licks of light,/bellows at the mountains,/fleeces snow to scatter,/frost to sow like ashes,/flings crumbs of hail so cold/no one can stand the sting,/then shifts from freeze to thaw/with wet and melting winds!/Such a God speaks to you/in law and living rule!/To no one else! God speaks/commands to no one else!" The storm becomes a different icon of relationship in each psalm.

We may accept from these psalms that both God and God's earth know one another in the risks of creation and destruction. Or we may not. We may be so overwhelmed by contemporary destruc-

⁷My reworking from Dahood's basic translations.

168

tiveness that we can see those psalms only as some sort of lovely wordplay which worsens today's tragedy instead of salving it. Even the images of death in the psalms are cinematic, "You drew me up/like water from the well/of Death, O God!" (Psalm 30); "I was near death/ . . . God stooped into the slime,/hauled me back up/ . . ."(Psalm 40); "Death will crow if it wins,/I ate him up!" (Psalm 13); "You did not surrender/me to Death to/walk its endless reaches." (Psalm 31); "I sprawl like a/battlefield corpse in a fresh grave,/you forget where/you buried it, you feel nothing." (Psalm 88); "Do not order us back/to the slime of the earth." (Psalm 90); ". . . Great God, free me, I am no match/for Death when it hunts;/spring me from its prison . . ." (Psalm 142). We may in fact . . . want all images to expire between ourselves and whatever is ultimately real so we live or die without illusion. We may want to say to God with Psalm 39, "Forget who I am. Let me/be glad I lived. Then/let me die and do not know." The grip of the psalmist on God with those lines is knuckle white! The emptiness itself has become an image. Without an image through which to relate, the divine and the human both become nothing to one another.

The lines of the psalmist match, therefore, the paradox in those who live a spirituality that is based on imagination. They want to cling to the divine without being tormented by the divine, cling to the human without being tormented by the human. And equally, they want the divine to cling to divinity without being tormented, and cling the same way to humanity. And that sets up a ferocious demand on their imaginations, to create images, or to respond to images, that will allow the integrity of relationship just described, which will not blink the destructiveness, nor curse the creativeness and die. There is also a ferocious demand on them to re-envision traditional images for their life-giving or death-dealing behavior, not a bowdlerizing, but a real entertaining, a truth labeling. All the images will be kept, but they will be known in themselves for what they are. So it is really not an expiration of images that these people want, but an expiration of the false claims that images have borne, or been made to bear, e.g., this set has the only explanation of good; this set, the only explanation of evil, etc.

Some rules for the imagination have grown up among those who live the modern paradox: 1) the image that is created or entertained must be allowed to speak for itself. Any propaganda ruins the beauty of the image, and therefore the truth of it for divine/human relationship. It does not matter if the propaganda comes from an oppressed or oppressing person or class. The truth/beauty of an image is ruined if it is aimed at imposing or guaranteeing a response. Yet point of view is expected, for the image is an interpersonal creation in a specific time and place, that is what makes it unique and non-coercive. 2) The way of creating the image or being invited to create it, entertain it, is crucial. There cannot be a physical, technical fakery. There must be no aesthetic lie from within the creation or co-creation, i.e., hyper-expression which tricks the self and tricks the user. 3) The image, especially the religious image, must be free of sectarian control which shifts the experience of the image to the experience of the control over it. The image must be capable of its own mediation, however limited. 4) The image must possess its own beauty or its own testimony to beauty. The word beauty means the power the image has to present life from within itself. This cannot be extrinsic to the image or the image is suborned. 5) The beauty must be a free gift of itself to someone who is left free in receiving it. Only this way can the image be a primary creator of relationship. 6) The qualities of the spiritual relationship derive from the qualities found in the image. The divine and the human now live in a mutual love of the image that unites them, a passionate love when the image is free, a compassionate love when the image is not. 7) Respect for the act of creation reveals the destiny the divine and the human have with one another. These conditions seem to be laid on the imagination. They are not imperious demands made beforehand. They come well after the experience of deceiving and being deceived by images, and well into the attempt to undo the deception.

There is a new dignity in the human voice toward the divine. That voice is in conflict with old voices that had to pretend *lèse majesté* in order to speak—the liturgical language of self-effacement before the sovereign. There is a new dignity to what that voice tells the divine. There is the implication that the divine so respects the human that it waits to be told, and the human senses this, so it reveals both the sorrow and the joy to a God who must listen if that God is to know. There is a new dignity to the human love offerred to the divine. It is an erotic love; it is not ashamed; it is an openess to the divine that is like a physical nakedness. Equally, there is a new dignity in the divine voice toward the human. It is a voice of truth without power, a voice that depends entirely on the love it has and the truth it knows. There is a new dignity to what the divine tells the human. The divine has lived by free choice all that the human has done, in knowledge when the human has shared it, in ignorance when the human has not, but in a deathless way, without escape. There is a new dignity to the divine love offerred to the human. It too is erotic love and like a nakedness, but there is a scope to this nakedness that is like the scope of space around the earth.

Poetry has been working out a language for these new dignities for some time now. There is the language born out of trench warfare and fratricidal struggle—the image of war as eating shit.[8] There is the language of the *avant garde* tradition which tried to restore liberty to form in the era of fascism—the image of pure play as the only sense.[9] There is the language grown of the worst of horrors, the Holocaust, language that tries to tell God and humankind what they both lost when the victims were incinerated—the image of the victim teaching divinity to God, humanity to killers. [10] There is the language born of womanhood discovering its own ways of being sacred—the image of being sister to the divine and the human.[11] There is the language born of an intense love of unspoiled nature, a whole-earth mindfulness—the image of the mothering earth.[12] There is the language born out of liturgical shambles in various religious traditions; it is a profane language trying to revive a sacred corpse mouth to mouth—the image of the anonymous believer.[13] There is the

[8]Cf. Paul Fussell, *The Great War And Modern Memory* (New York: Oxford University Press, 1975).

[9]Cf. Jerome Rothenberg, *The Revolution Of The Word* (New York: Seabury, 1974).

[10]Cf. Elie Wiesel, *Ani-maamin: A Song Lost And Found Again* (New York: Random House, 1974). *The Trial Of God* (New York: Random House, 1979).

[11]Cf. Adrienne Rich, *Poems: Selected And New* (New York: Norton, 1975). Robin Morgan, *The Lady Of The Beasts* (New York: Random House, 1976).

[12]Cf. Gary Snyder, *Turtle Island* (New York: New Directions, 1974).

[13]Cf. Ramon Guthrie, *Maximum Security Ward* (New York: Farrar, Straus & Giroux, 1970).

language borne of the lyric soul that has learned to sing the difference between itself and its political captor—the image of the survivor.[14] Lastly, there is the language born of a sexual hunger for God through every sensual shape of the earth—the image of wrestling all night with God for orgasm, not for power.[15] It is not that a single person or single poem has made the new language for the new voice; to each sentence above several names could be attached. It is that a harvest of dignity is possible from the many poets who have tried to make poetry not "a lying word," concerned only with prettying itself up for display, and not something to deride later when poetry has made "nothing happen," but a truth to live by, an act of creation which reveals what human beings must all be like to live and not die from one another.

[14]Cf. Eugenia Ginzburg, *Within The Whirlwind* (New York: Harcourt, Brace, 1981).

[15]Cf. William Everson, *River Root: A Syzygy* (Berkeley: Oyez, 1976). *The Masks Of Drought* (Santa Barbara: Black Sparrow Press, 1980).

[16]Mitchel Dahood, *Op. Cit.,* vol. 2.

ORATORIO FOR AN APOCALYPSE

Prenote:

I wrote the Oratorio which follows at the request of a composer. The composer accepted the text, then did not do the music for it because of outside reasons, reasons I found very convincing. I put the text away for a while before deciding to try to get it published as a poem. Later, I submitted it to a religious journal whose editor thought I was playing games with words. I lost my confidence in it then, I must admit. A few years later, however, during my correspondence with another editor, Burton Raffel of *The Denver Quarterly*, I referred to the text saying to him I thought it showed what way my imagination worked with religious material. I asked him if he would like to see it. He had just accepted to publish some other poems of mine and we were corresponding about religious poetry. He was more than willing to look at the Oratorio. He read it and wrote me very quickly back that he wanted to publish it as well as the poems since it did represent to him an example of incarnational imagination. In fact, he was enthusiastic about the text, and his enthusiasm restored it for me in a wonderful way. After the poem was published in the summer of 1977, I offered it only one more time, as part of the Arrington Lectures I gave in the fall of 1977 at Sewanee, to the School of Theology. Then I put it aside until another chance happening, a conversation with the publisher of this volume, Virgil Funk, about images of the 'end time.' He asked if I lived with any sense of Apocalypse which affected my life and creativity. I said I did, but it was not of a destructive kind like the Book of Revelations. I mentioned my Oratorio and he, in his turn, asked to see it. After he read it, he suggested that I include it in this volume of poetic psalms and explanatory essays. I am happy to do so because this text is the one in which I worked out my hopes for my own life and for the lives of others. It is both a poem and a creed. It is the primary influence on everything in this volume.

One more historical note. After I finished writing it in the fall of 1973, I went to New York to hear an Oratorio by Elie Wiesel, *Animaamin: A Song Lost And Found Again*, music by Darius Milhaud. His Oratorio was magnificent, a poetic theology of rare beauty and truthfulness. I knew I had a different imagination than Wiesel's. His work, nevertheless, was such a freeing experience of imagination dealing with disaster that, by a paradox which often happens through art, I loved the difference between us more after that evening in Carnegie Hall. My loss of confidence came later. I

174

often teach Wiesel's Oratorio. I now feel that I can ask people to look again at my own. I think that there is a feeling around that 'visions of the end' are so stark that they stop all creativity in both personal and communal life. My Oratorio is a belief that creativity cannot be stopped, that it can begin from nothing over and over again. The belief grows from my experience of the way incarnational images work, in poetry, in religion.

ORATORIO FOR AN APOCALYPSE

(from the center of darkness)

Narrator:
I heard love songs lost in crowds,
crowds like stands of forest in gale
winds, and the love songs were snapping
like branches, and the earth was covered
with their windfall, but the love songs
kept starting again despite the warnings,
beautiful sounds the screech of the wind
kept breaking, men and women breaking.

(from the center of growing light)

Voice 1:
I hold your voice in my hands,
drops out of fog,
out of rain from you drumming
my skin like baying
hounds who catch the scent of
my cloth, your voice,
your love in a coat of fool's
bells I steal
each night to keep you from
the harm of owls,
from buzzard highway lamps who
never know names
for their food but carrion's luck,
your voice that rubs
night clean of me and falls.

(from the center of growing light)

Voice 2:
Dark and lovely and gone,
sold for haunches,
you, my love, made meat,
bid for, taken
from me, and I the animal
because I whimpered;
the hat you put on the sun

176

forgotten for your teeth;
the wine of the goatskin moon
you drank with a laugh
forgotten for teeth and the heat
your skull might stand;
I sing a loon's grief in your trees
that are charred to shoes
for the dead, you lovely, you gone!

(from the center of crowded light)

Voice 3:
Green smoke has no way to rub
the lilacs from
your eyes; when the trumpet
comes I will know
your bones in the heap they made;
I will be winds
meanwhile to stir the dust
of you alive
as ginger pervading the room
where you put roses
and set hot bread under linen
cloth and lighted
lilacs in your eyes to turn
our prayers to you
with your purple, dancing flames!

(from spots in a dying light)

Voice 1:
She was snow bending grass
over cradles of larks.

Chorus:
Shake, shake the snow free!
Grass is silage;
sickles sing the lasting song
ringing stones.

Voice 2:
She was stitches of rain;
she healed faces.

Chorus:
Seed clouds! The eyes of needles

are tumbleweed
choking useless fields
with dead hair.

Voice 3:
She poured tea from her pain;
she set me cups.

Chorus:
Her blood tainted our stream;
filter it out!

Feed the buzzards carrion!
Stamp all meat!
Watch every stream for spots
that mar our sun!

(confusion creating silence, darkness)

(from the center of silence, darkness)

Narrator:
I heard the beginning of rain
at night on the desert's roof
during the sleep of the wind
when my eyes forgot the light
and were futile as the breasts
of a man, as a woman's fists;
it was someone come from silence
to unlock the air itself from
the corpse of its fixed shout,
to make it be young as a wind
out naming flowers new names
in a game of blind man's buff;
and morning heard of the game
and came with careful thunder
to sit on old fences and watch.
I did not know who he was;
I knew his song; the same song!

(from the center of growing light)

Christus:
I will be water for you;
I will leap from rock cliffs
in falls for your drought.

Chorus:
You will spatter on rocks
like the promise of spit, useless
to cure our wilderness.
We ran to you once with cups
circling beneath you like thirsty
fools caught in a fog
with only punctured hats
to catch us a mouthful of water;
it fanned into rainbows for our eyes
but fled from our thirst;
all love flees from us with
the rattle of the dying!
Look at our empty cups!
Look at our fool's dance
for water, for ghost water!

Christus:
I will be new seed for you;
I will be the end of winter,
a wind that comes back.

Chorus:
Too many mouths eat the earth;
too much love increases its weight;
we smother in paradise,
in multitudes of arms and legs,
where we thought to find joy.
The womb is a bottle of flies
we stir up with our love;
it is not the song we thought it,
the song of the piper sitting in
a tree who watches gorgeous sunsets
through spare branches.
Joy is a trick, not a treat;
we turn into pumpkins with grins.
A new spring makes a yellow fall
with too many wicked grins.

Christus:
I will write mercy in the dust;
I will play you mercy
on keys of dust.

Chorus:
Mercy is a knife at our throats;
you put a knife to our throats.
Mercy is a lamb that forgets
the snow is not fleece, not milk;
it is the switchblade of innocence
that kills lambs out to play.
The flesh's juices all may run
when the way home is nothing
but a look and a game of silence;
love can be thrown as a ball
at bottles in a carnival for
a stuffed bear or a dime's loss.
Mercy makes love a lot full of trash
where no homes can be built,
where good money pours after bad.

Christus:
Yes, I am wheat caught fire;
no, not charnel house bones;
yes, an eagle outstaring the sun!

Chorus:
We burned your cross on their lawn;
they came back.
We flew your skull and bones,
and they did not die.
We put them out to freeze;
we put them in circles of hell;
we tacked tails of damnation
on their doors and awaited angels
to exact penalty with a sure sword;
but every word you said lodged
in our throats like a ball of thorns.
The heathen still suckle their gods.
Send your fire down now
before it is too late
and our swords turn to noonday wax!

(from the center of fitful light)

(Improperia)

Christus:
You twisted my dance, made it
a noose for my neck;

180

what did I do but draw linen
blue sky in yards
to cure the milk in your eyes;
you knotted the sky,
made it a mushroom halter,
turned me to a jig
of dry bones out hustling love
for nickels and dimes,
turned my heart to a skull
choking on bones.

Chorus:
Blood in our veins is better
than truth in your corpse;
it was you or the noonday sun!

Christus:
I told you faces were mornings
coloring rainfall;
I told you breasts were pity,
were bows of moons;
I told you wombs were like waves
laughing ashore,
that hair wiped away death,
and tears were lightning
splitting the sky with one stroke;
what did I do
when I drew you a kingdom of flesh
you sold by the piece.

Chorus:
You need to sell flesh! No flesh,
no sale! Hunger
knows what soothes raw gums!

Christus:
The screams rise, the bodies
fall; the flames
rise, the hands fall;
the shouts rise,
the heads fall; the hammers
rise, the nails,
the nails, the sparrows fall;
the lilies, the sun,
the children, the hills fall;

181

you beg the hills
to fall; but I loved you!
What did I do!

Chorus:
Love is sure death; the game
is king of the mountain
or stiffs for the mangle of hell!

Christus:
You make each word a clam
with mud for meat;
my love that scours the tides
in spring will starve;
you tell me sand is gold,
the wind is trust,
the waves a ring for my finger;
my love is flesh
and blood I place in your hands
like a birth; what
did I do that you feed me
clams full of mud!

(from the center of light and darkness)

Narrator:
I saw bottom sky at night crawling
with stars: I saw survivors fall from
the blackened hull of the dark, dropping
with exhausted arms; each one flared red
as it struck the atmosphere; I heard voices
from inside them pleading do something!
do something! do! but an answer
like monotone pity said over and over
nothing to do! nothing! air burns! air!
My head was filled with their voices
clashing do! do! nothing! nothing!
Then my flesh shivered like cymbals,
it fell at my feet and whimpered!

(from spots in a dying light)

Christus:
My last seed is gone;
it is glass on desert gravel
striking at the sun!

Chorus:
No! One more! Melt the glass!

Christus:
My last egg is gone
from the vine; my last blood
dries on my hand!

Chorus:
No! One more! Shake the vine!

Christus:
My last look is gone;
I curl up in flames like paper
swallowing tongues!

Chorus:
No! One more! Open the grate!

Christus:
My last word is gone;
turned to a smoking stump
with one bolt!

Chorus:
No! No! We cannot be glass,
be spit in the dirt, be dead fire!
Tear bellies open for another egg!
Root in the desert for another seed!
Pull the pole of the tent of the sky,
there is the seed, there are the looks!
Do not burn! Do something, something!

(confusion creating silence, darkness)

(from the center of visible darkness)

Narrator:
I saw then a field full of people
still as death; each one who spoke
killed a man; each one who moved
struck someone down, the least song,
the least look struck someone down;
they fell silent; they stopped each other;
they sat fierce as death.
But one voice broke out;
it did not kill; I heard their frenzy
to become the voice that did not kill.

(from a start of light)

Christus:
The stones sing out where the dead cannot!

(from a stop of light)

Chorus:
Yes! Sing a song of stones! He says it!
Let our corpses go! The gates of hell
will not prevail against a song of stones!
Let our corpses go! Pick up stones!
Pick up lasting songs! Lasting!

(from a start of light)

Christus:
Wheat will grow where the dead cannot;
dust will love where the dead cannot;
ashes will rise to dance for an empty wind!

(from a stop of light)

Chorus:
Yes! Turn to dust and ashes! He says it!
In the mouth, in the ears, in the eyes,
in the nostrils, in our hands dust and ashes!
World, come tumbling down, He says it!
Empty each wind for the dancing dust!

(from a start of light)

Christus:
Love straightens twisted hearts!
It is fierce as fire, a storm in the sun!

(from a stop of light)

Chorus:
Yes! Burn sinners in bundles!
Hold the cross to their last lips;
Let them see the kingdom to come
as their hearts twist straight in the fire!
Clear the earth for love with the sun!

(from a start of light)

Christus:
If you knew, if you knew my love!

(from a stop of light)

Chorus:
Yes! Who is not with you is
against you! We have millstones ready!
We have acres of darkness. We have
keys; we unlock bread for the worthy!
We are your love in the face of the earth
from the rise of the sun to its going!

(darkness stops the light, and makes silence)

(from the center of darkness)

Narrator:
In the silence after the frenzy of death,
I heard his voice begin again, and at it,
both grief and joy harrowed my soul.
I saw some in the field with a song for a face.
I saw some in the field with a storm for a face.
They could not see one another, could not hear;
only his sound, the song or the storm of silence.

(from the center of light and darkness)

Christus:
In a careless rain,
in a careless love,
thistles will grow
and rocks be blind
to the fall of the rain.

In a careless moon,
in a careless love,
blood will sing
and dogs will yelp
to the fall of the light.

Pain is tea or
a mouthful of scald
in a careless love;
a kiss is grace or
a howling hell
in a careless love;
a heart is a scourge,
a heart is a strum,
is a hood or a hat
in a careless love.

I love the rain;
I love the moon;
I love what grows;
I love what sings

with a careless love;

I love the tea;
I love the kiss;
I love the heart;
I love the strum

with a careless love.

POSTSCRIPT

Apocalypses flourish when human values seem closest to defeat, especially human values taught by religious beliefs. Can God be wrong? Can we who believe in God be wrong if evil succeeds? Where no God gave the human values, the questions are just as sharp. Is our law too weak? And our customs unable to deal with barbarism in or outside ourselves? No, says Apocalypse. This is what will happen in a future you cannot see, when the truth you believe in will prevail. Good will triumph and in this way, by destroying evil, whatever the evil may be. Believers will never be troubled again. They will enjoy forever the values that they fear are being destroyed now. For non-believers, law, custom, sheer humanity will break through terror itself and be victorious for so long as human being will last. There may be few or many believers to reach the final triumph, few or many humanists. No matter, the good will vanquish the evil.

I have found the christian Apocalypse to be vindictive and destructive, in itself, and in the use made of it by my tradition. So I started work on my Oratorio with a desire to find a new image or images which would lead me toward what I called a mature innocence, the kind that wants to save experience, not destroy it—something like the catacomb image of Jesus the Good Shepherd carrying a goat instead of a sheep into green pastures. I did not want to impose meanings borrowed from previous Apocalyptic imagery on what I was to write. It really happened that way, my starting out with such an image, not knowing where the image would lead, but desiring keenly that it might lead to a mature innocence. The first image was nonverbal. I drew, instinctively, two up-curving lines,)), then a horizontal line, —, then a down-curving line, (, next an up-curving line,), then a horizontal line seeming to stretch forever ————. As I meditated that diagram,)) — ( ) ————, a sense of realities beginning from nothing and rising to climaxes where they are destroyed began to appear. Still without verbal content. Realities beginning from nothing, apparently, over and over, and being destroyed. Then the analogy to a love song gave me my first hint about language to interpret the design, and about all that I hoped would accompany language: 1) the rich, sensual tone found in the Apocalypse, however slaughterous the imagery itself proved to be later, 2) the many levels of experience from separate times and places that could be joined, 3) the chance even that language could contain in its pronunciation the word stresses that evoke the esoteric number symbolism the Apocalypse is so spendthrift about, fours, threes, eights, sevens, combinations of these, 4) then the feeling that human knowledge can be in touch with the guiding forces underlying creation itself.

I hoped the love song would be able to resist continually the temptation to be a righteous avenger. The love song would be able to respond to some*one*, some*thing* loved, even if the other were a killer kind, animate or inanimate. Any revenge, any pure punition, any wiping away, and the love song would change in its inward self to a Horst Wessel/Onward Christian Soldiers/hymn. The love song would be a continual revelation of the truth of creation, and would only be a lie if creation became, in its entirety, evil and spawning evil—to use non-love song language. Ultimately, the love song would need no sanction from a God or a culture to possess and to live out its truth. That is a lesson poetry itself teaches me. The Oratorio begins with love songs that withstand the temptation to become rightous avengers. They owe their strength only to human truth. So I feel. The first upward motion needs no God, no culture to make it real. The first upward motion is destroyed by both religion and culture, and there is silence.

The second upward motion has the Christus figure suffused with the truth of the love song sung in the first movement. It is as if he appears within the truth and makes it glow more—or she, because the Christus is alternately man and woman in this second creation leading up to a second destruction. The Christus voice is small, three lines four times, the seven of creation awaiting the eighth day which is eternity. The anti-voice, the song of hate, occurs in fifteen lines four times, fifteen being the union of eight and seven, but gone awry so that time imprisons eternity. The hate in this upward motion is the hate born of frustration, the sort that comes to those who use ideals for selfish purposes, whose hate is understandable up to a point, but not understandable when inflicted on life with lethal consequences. Such hate originates in despair, in excessive suffering. For each anti-voice, the voice of the Christus supplies the vision that causes the antipathy, i.e., altruism, grace, mercy, lasting life in family form.

The third motion is like a horizon line. The Christus becomes the horizon that does not depart, that stays present to all variations of the living earth. The Christus is here the accumulation of that truth of human love found in the first motion, and that truth which he/she made his/her own in the conflicts of a single lifetime, within a single culture, in a single place. In the second motion, there is

189

really a colloquy between the historical Christus and other times than his own. In the third, the colloquy is between a pervasive Christus and a pervasive human reality. The form of the colloquy is that of an ancient liturgy, improperia, or complaints, medieval complaints of the Christus to the people watching the passion of his love song in a loveless way. The imagery is modern. The attempt I made was to find images that could absorb, without bursting, three moments, the moment of meaning in the original Christus, the unresolved barbarism of modern life, and an illumination of the two in the voice of a medieval liturgical figure before a congregation. The verse stress, as in previous segments, is three, two, repeatedly, so as to fall short of any symbolic number of consequence, that way indicating a fruitless search for completion. The stanzaic form has, in its twelve/three ratio, another purpose. The numbers are right, twelve/three leading to fifteen, which is eight, eternity, seven, time, in union, but the struggle is lifted onto the plane of meaning. And there the Christus voice is destroyed by the willed response of the chorus, the anti-voice, though all the structures are right for harmony. Each of the *improperia* can be sung by a man or a woman, and each is a love song in the complaint style.

The fourth motion is a downward curve. Its main purpose is to intensify the death of the horizon motion. It seems as if the Christus can be totally destroyed. And that anti-Christus recognizes this. But is unable to stop the effects of hate, and knows it, and is reduced to a frenzied contradiction of itself in order to save itself. There are four three-line songs for the Christus, four one-line responses. The perfection of creation remains in him/her, while creation is monovalent in the response. However, in the final response to the Christus, here, the anti-voice has seven lines, pleading for life against its own self, which marks the most intense point of the contradiction in hate.

The fifth motion is an upward curve again, a beginning from nothing, a rising again to a climax of destruction. The corner has been turned and the anti-voice realizes its survival depends on the Christus. This was the most painful part for me to write because this movement describes the way christian religion of the Apocalypse, taken literally, behaves in its attempt to win eternity for itself from a Christus it thinks it understands. I mean all the confessions of christianity, my own as well as others. The Christus voice appears in one, three, two, and one lines, the seven of

perfect creation, the four of the earth alone. The anti-voice is ir-
regular. In the end, literal belief has cleared everyone out, Christus
and believers, for safety's sake.

The sixth motion is a beginning again, but there is no anti-voice.
This is the voice that does the *final judging*. It is not *final judging*. It is the love song of the Christus now perpetual. It is a sum-
mary of the love songs of the Oratorio, and is based upon a dual
understanding of the word "careless." Those who hear it one way
do not know love. Those who hear it another way do. And it is
always possible to hear it in the opposite way, so hearing is not
once for always. It is continual. The song does not yield to the
temptation to be a final avenger. The lines are two-stress, the stanzaic pattern fives, thus the number of perfect creation, seven,
which means earth, air, fire, water, plus the three-personed-God of
christian belief. The song itself is the human truth.

There is no seventh motion, no perfection to creation just before
entering the eighth day, the everlasting day. I cannot imagine a
greater human moment, or divine, than the love song of the
Christus, the one that seems perpetual now. I do not mean my
own version of it, but the one my own looks to. It is a tame vision
to be judged forever by a love song. To me it is the surest revelation of the truth of creation. I know its effects on me. The evening
I finished the last song my consciousness was sprung open, people
seemed to be talking like parrots, not communicating. My own
speech was disjointed. My senses were intensified. To think that
everything turns now on the love or hate one has for the forms of
creation, with or without benefit of religion or culture, that the
truth within creation is judgment without revenge, but judgment
surely, that every moment of immanent time has more importance
than the moments of transcendent time, broke the customary patterns of my mind for a while, so that I could see, briefly, the difference between ordinary and Apocalyptic time in the present of
my life.

I have left out Gospel revenge as unworthy of God or of
humankind. I have left out Gospel punition as unworthy of God or
humankind. I have stripped Gospel down to the compassion of
love and kept it within historical time as the lasting truth of God
and humankind. I have been taught to do this by someone who
knows the Gods of the cultures, Mircea Eliade, by someone who
knows the God of Judaism, Elie Wiesel, and by someone who
knows the God of Christianity, William Lynch.

Francis Patrick Sullivan is a Jesuit priest. He has published two volumes of poetry, *Table Talk With The Recent God* (Paulist Press, 1974) and *Spy Wednesday's Kind* (The Smith, 1979). He teaches courses on aesthetics and theology at Boston College and at the Gregorian University, Rome. He received a MacDowell Colony residency in the summer of 1982 to complete work on *Lyric Psalms*.

Aileen Callahan is a member of the fine arts faculties of Boston College and Regis College. She received an M.F.A. in painting from Boston University and studied at the Escuela Nacional de Pinture y Escultura, Mexico, (Lincoln Scholar two years) and Skowhegan School of Painting and Sculpture. Her murals and other works are in collections in the United States and Mexico.